MW00531851

THE CURIOUS HISTORY OF

WEIGHTS & MEASURES

THE CURIOUS HISTORY OF

WEIGHTS & MEASURES

Claire Cock-Starkey

BODLEIAN
LIBRARY
PUBLISHING

First published in 2023 by the Bodleian Library
Broad Street, Oxford OX1 3BG
www.bodleianshop.co.uk

ISBN 978 1 85124 579 6

Publisher: Samuel Fanous
Managing Editor: Susie Foster
Editor: Janet Phillips
Picture Editor: Leanda Shrimpton
Cover design by Dot Little at the Bodleian Library
Designed and typeset by Lucy Morton of illuminati
in 10½ on 14 Baskerville
Printed and bound in China by C&C Offset Printing Co., Ltd.
on 120 gsm Chinese Baijin Pure woodfree paper

British Library Catalogue in Publishing Data
A CIP record of this publication is available from the British Library

CONTENTS

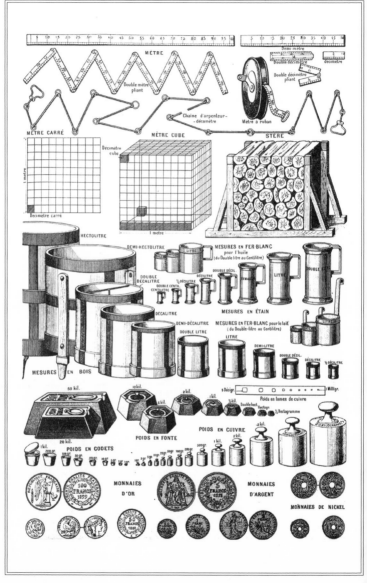

INTRODUCTION

In evidence given to Parliament's 1862 Select Committee on Weights and Measures, a Mr Greenall remarked on the extraordinary number of different historical weights and measures in use at that time across Britain, listing the grain, dram, drop, ounce, pound, stone, score, ton; the wool measure of clove, tod, wey, pack, sack or last; the straw measure of truss and load; the draper's measure of inch, nail, ell and yard; the long measure and land measure of line, size, hand, foot, palm, span, pace, step, link, knot, rood, hide, rod, pole or perch, fall, chain, mile and league; plus various other scales of measurement including the strike, peck, pot, gill, pint, quart, tierce, boll, coomb, pipe, butt, tun and score. This impressive array of customary measurements not only shows the plethora of competing and coexisting weights and measures in Britain but also reveals the innate human desire to create order. Every sector of industry saw fit to develop its own method to assess weight, length, volume or area, attesting to the importance of measurement in trade and commerce. What Mr Greenall's list also reveals (and here I must confess that I edited his list because it is so long; what you see above is not the gamut of measures!) is that by the mid-nineteenth century more and more voices were advocating that we call time on the myriad measures. Those bastions of Victorian life, science, industry and rational thought, demanded a consolidation of measurements. But how did we get to this point? How and why did all these different measures develop? And what has made some persist to this day, while others have fallen from use?

Protagoras (*c.*490–420 BCE), according to Plato, once observed that 'man is the measure of all things'; the long history of anthropocentric measurements would indicate that he wasn't wrong. The very earliest measures did not rely on scales and values but instead on comparison. And what better thing with which to compare the length of an item than an always-to-hand body part. Fingernails, fingers, palms, forearms, feet, paces and body spans have all been put to good use as the simplest form of measurement. Likewise weight could be judged through comparison with a good-sized stone. These basic but effective methods of measurement were successfully employed for many hundreds of years the world over. However, as trade increased, and with it the need for regulation and taxation, it became increasingly important that, on a local level at least, standard measures be enforced. In this way most sectors of industry, from cloth-makers to jewellers, developed their own standard measures. Rather unhelpfully they frequently adopted a known customary measure, such as the stone, and then adapted it to their needs. This meant that while widely used across Britain, the stone had a confusing variety of values from region to region, sector to sector. To return to Mr Greenall's evidence, he explained that

> A stone of wool sold by the growers is 14 lbs., while that sold by wool-staplers to each other is 15 lbs.; a stone of wool at Darlington is 18 lbs., while at Belfast it is 16¾ lbs. A stone of flax at Downpatrick is 24 lbs., and a stone of flax at Belfast is not only 16¾ lbs, but it is also 24½ lbs., so that it has two values in one town.

Evidence such as this made it clear that this confusing array of localized measures could not continue and order needed to be called.

The Enlightenment saw the dawning of scientific method and rational thought. Old superstitious ideas were jettisoned as reason now demanded that all knowledge be backed up with evidence. But to conduct thorough experiments accurate measures are required. No longer was weighing something against the local lump of stone accepted. Measurement, it was argued, should now be based on immutable natural laws. William Thomson, Baron Kelvin, in his presidential address to the British Association for the Advancement of Science in 1871, summed up the importance of standardized, scientific measures:

> Accurate and minute measurement seems to the non-scientific imagination, a less lofty and dignified work than looking for something new. But nearly all the grandest discoveries of science have been but the rewards of accurate measurement and patient long-continued labour in the minute sifting of numerical results.

This move towards rational thought spelled the end for our cluttered and confusing customary measures and started the race towards an international system of measures based on natural laws rather than physical objects. *The Curious History of Weights & Measures* traces a wider history by examining the individual stories behind measurements, both old and new, current and outmoded. The book is organized into five sections: weight; length; volume; culinary and informal measures; scales and scores.

In the weight section the earliest forms of weighing, based on items close at hand – a grain of barley or a large stone – are considered. From here I discuss the development of the troy, apothecaries' and avoirdupois systems, which were superseded by

Usage des Nouvelles Mesures.

imperial and then metric measures. Ultimately this section charts the move from a variety of sector-specific measures to international standards, which have taken us to the point where science has moved on to such an extent that many households now own an accurate weighing scale. This allows items to be measured against standard weights that are based on natural laws. Happily most measures are now so universal that consumers can be sure that if they purchase a 1 kg bag of flour in any country in the world it will weigh exactly the same.

The length section begins with anthropocentric measures, detailing how since antiquity various body parts have provided useful comparative measures. Naturally the confusion comes when a small child describes an item to their very tall father as a foot long, and each party considers the item as long as their own foot. More accurate and standard measures only grew in importance as international trade flourished and land began to be enclosed. Trade in cloth drove the need for standard and easily repeatable measures of length. This ensured not only that merchants were paid a fair price for their goods but also that the correct taxation could be charged. Similarly, since the twelfth century, the enclosure of land, whereby common land such as fields and meadows was divided up into individually owned plots of farmland, made accurate land measurements more pressing. These changes instigated more centrally controlled systems of measurement, overseen by the monarch or government, and saw the development of actual physical standards of length. These 'standards' were carefully crafted from metal and kept in the seat of power. From these standards further copies were made which could be sent out to each region, ensuring some level of national consensus.

When conceiving of larger distances, greater measures were required. These bigger measures, into which many smaller measures fell as subdivisions,

T Wharton & Compy

Taylors, Drapers &c,

Castle Court, Cornhill,

LONDON.

DIRECTIONS FOR MEASURING.

Coats.

1 Exact height of Person........

2 Round the Breast close under
  the Arms..................

3 Round the Waist..............

4 From the back seam between
  the Shoulders in a direct line
  to the Elbow the Arm forming
  a Square.....................

5 From the Elbow to the Hand ....

Waistcoats.

1 Pass a Tape behind the Neck
  (under the Coat) bringing it
  down on each Shoulder to meet
  at the bottom of the Waistcoat
  half of which will be the length required

2&3 Same as for Coat ....

Breeches.

1 Height of Person as before............

2 Length of the leg seam.. ....

3 Round the Waist under the Waistcoat

4 Round the Thigh ....

5 The Knee Band ....

EXAMPLE.

Coats.		Waistcoats.	
1	5 Feet 10 Inches	1	25 Inches........
2	40....	2	40..........
3	36 ½......	3	36 ½ ....
4	21 ½......		
5	13 ¾......		

Breeches.

1	5 Feet 10 Inches
2	18 ½.....
3	32......
4	22 ¼....
5	13........

The Measure may be taken on the above plan by
any Person using a Broad Tape & then applying
it to a scale of Inches & half Inches, to ascertain the
exact length, please to take Measure as noted on
the Figure, having the Coat buttoned.

Habits to be measured upon the same principle as a Coat.

Eng by M S Innes 23, Little Bell Alley near the Bank.

took the concept of length further away from its relationship with the human body. Knowing how far London is from Cambridge does not make it any closer, but through consistent use of the same large measures it allows people to visualize how far distant a location is and how long it will take them to get there. Concepts of distance have changed greatly over the years as modes of transport have improved and international travel has become more accessible. Indeed, our knowledge of the infinite size of space and the vast distances involved when thinking about the universe has seen our internal mental maps grow far bigger than was necessary hundreds of years ago, when travel to the local market town was the furthest most ordinary people would ever have to contemplate.

The volume section traces how our understanding of volume has changed over the years. The concept can be a tricky one to get your head around. This is because it relates not to the physical heft of something, but rather to the amount of space a substance takes up. This makes the calculation of volume a mathematical problem. In Ancient Greece the mathematical leap required for the everyday person on the street to actually calculate volume was avoided by creating standard vessels, known as amphorae, of various sizes which could hold standard amounts of goods. The archaeological record attests to a variety

of different-sized amphorae that were standardized regionally. The typical amphora had two handles and was used to transport oil, wine, grain or milk. A hydria was a three-handled vessel used only for storing and carrying water. Two of the handles were for carrying while the third was used to steady the vessel while pouring. Using vessels as a measure meant a numeric value did not need to be given to the volume inside; instead it was based on the capacity of a set container. This method of understanding volume was used across many cultures worldwide.

Customary units of volume differed across Europe, but in Britain the pint was the standard small measure. Trade in wine and ale caused large volumes to be defined in terms of huge barrels, while the small amounts of liquid used by apothecaries when dispensing medicines meant that it was this sector which first developed the smallest liquid measures. It was only really with the advent of metrification, first in France in the eighteenth century and later in

Britain in the 1970s, that standard, accurate measures of volume became commonplace. Litres and millilitres became scalable volumes, which could be used to conceptualize everything from a tiny teaspoon of liquid right up to a swimming pool full of water. For most people today, although we might regularly use litres and millilitres, when cooking we might struggle to picture what that volume of liquid actually looks like. Although we might now have standardized scales with which to describe volume, most people will still understand the volume of a liquid by picturing the container in which it is kept. Thus, when it comes to volume the container and its capacity still best describe the amount of any liquid.

When thinking and writing about measurement I did not want to simply focus on the mathematical or regulatory efforts which made modern measurements possible. I also wanted to look at some of the more inexact, archaic or informal measurements we all use in everyday life. Culinary measures sum up this desire perfectly. Here are a range of measurements that most cooks will understand in a tangible way but that have no real official classification. Similarly there are a whole host of sector-specific customary measures, such as the baker's dozen or the diamond carat, which saw a somewhat niche development. This heterogeneous section tries to address the history and stories behind some of the measurements which didn't find a logical home in the weight, length or volume sections.

The final section is concerned with scales and scores. There is something comforting and solid about a carefully created scale. Things seem immediately easier to process when we can assign a score or number to something. Unsurprisingly many of the most familiar scientific scales relate to measuring the impact of a natural disaster. The chaos, damage and danger produced by an earthquake or tornado can seem partially tamed when given a score and ranked against previous disasters.

The primary function of scales and scores is to make them easily comparable with other similar events, objects or effects. The score can be reassuring – 'Oh phew, the earthquake was only 4 on the Richter scale' – or perhaps present an excuse to brag – 'I ate a chilli pepper with a Scoville score of 100,000 SHU' – but some, such as the Bristol stool scale, can also provide a format to communicate a delicate matter to your doctor more effectively.

Officially in statistics there are four types of scale: nominal, ordinal, interval and ratio. The scales become more detailed and complex as they go up in order. A nominal scale is very basic and serves to simply label or name something. For example, a familiar nominal scale is the list of ethnicities included with most forms these days. You can only select one answer and no score is generated; instead you are just labelling yourself as an ethnicity. Nominal scales are useful for recording simple information. With ordinal scales it is the order of the scales which is important. Ordinal scales are useful for classifying information which can be measured against other options but for which there is no exact measure between items. For example, a happiness scale is ordinal. We know that happy is higher up the scale than unhappy but the exact measurement between the two is not known. Interval scales are the most frequently used type of scale featured in this section. They are numeric scales where we know the order and the exact difference between each of the values on the scale. Temperature scales are a classic example of interval scales. The one problem with interval scales, in terms of statistical modelling, is that they have no absolute zero – as in a zero which has no value. In a temperature scale zero has a value, as do negative numbers; this means that you cannot calculate ratios. To solve this there is the final type of statistical scale: the ratio scale. These types of scale have an order: we know the exact measurement between each rung on the scale and they have an absolute zero. This means statisticians can do all sorts of whizzy maths with them such as calculating ratios and averages.

This history of weights and measures does not attempt to tell the story of every measure ever known. Instead I hope my careful selection of the most interesting stories will provide an engaging overview and shed some light on the human desire for order, the development of regulation, the growth of international trade, the impact of science and rational thought, and the push for standardization. *The Curious History of Weights & Measures* is Anglocentric in scope; so, other than a few references, it does not delve into the fascinating complexities of the numerous systems of weights and measures developed across China, Japan, India, Africa and the Middle East. I shall leave you to dive in (or dip in and out, if you prefer) with a final thought from Plato:

> If someone separated the art of counting and
> measuring and weighing from all the other arts,
> what was left of each [of the others] would be, so to
> speak, insignificant.

Weights—*continued*.

Iron Bell, Bar and Flat Weights, in dozens.
(Plugged and Adjusted).

1550

1552	1556

¼	½	1	2	4	7	14	28	56 lbs.
1/10	2/3	3/6	6/-	9/6	15/-	24/-	44/-	84/- per doz.

1554

Iron Round or Square Ring Weights
in dozens. (Plugged and Adjusted).

¼	½	1	2	4	7	14lbs.
2/3	2/9	4/9	7/3	11/-	17/-	26/-

28	56 lbs.
48/-	88/- per doz.

Nett Extra for Stamping Weights.

Flat Weights, in sets 1 2 4 7 lbs. down

	4½d.	5½d.	7d.	9d. per set

Weights in dozens—

¼	½	1	2	4	8 ozs.
7d.	7d.	7d.	7d.	7d	7d.

1	2	4	7	14	28	56 lbs.
1/2	1/2	1/2	2/3	2/3	3/6	3/6 per doz.

Nett Extra for Stamping Scales.

1 lb.	..	..	..	3d. each.
Over 1 lb. to 14 lbs.	..	..	4d ,,
,, 14 lb. to 56 lbs	..	..	9d ,,

WEIGHTS

'It was a great step in science when men became convinced that, in order to understand the nature of things, they must begin by asking, not whether a thing is good or bad, noxious or beneficial, but of what kind it is? And how much is there of it?'

JAMES CLERK MAXWELL

Grain

Since antiquity various grains have been used as the smallest unit of weight, most often carob seeds, wheat or barley grains. Grains made a practical basis for measurement systems because they were readily available and were thought to be of a consistent weight. Traditionally 1 carob seed was said to be equivalent to 4 wheat grains or 3 barleycorns. Modern analysis, however, suggests that the weight of grains can be highly variable as they are so sensitive to soaking up moisture.

In the apothecaries', troy and avoirdupois systems the grain is the smallest unit of weight, and is based on the weight of a single grain of barley. Reflecting the long history of the grain as a unit of measure, it is the only unit of weight which has a consistent value across the three main historical British systems of measurement. In modern terms a grain weighs 64.79891 milligrams. Naturally, with British weights and measures there is one exception to this surprising consensus: in the Tower system a grain is based not on barley but on a single grain of wheat. A single wheat grain is lighter than a barley grain, which is traditionally considered 1⅓ the weight of a wheat grain.

Evidence from royal decrees dating back to as early as the eighth century suggests that in Britain

grains were used as the basis for the weight of money. One such decree from the thirteenth century defines an English penny in the Tower system as 'Thirty-two Grains of Wheat dry in the midst of the Ear'. In the troy system, used concurrently with the Tower system, an English penny was defined as 22.5 barley grains.

In early modern England the grain continued to be used to measure small amounts of goods, such as medicines, precious metals and coinage. The ubiquity of the grain is revealed by the fact that when the imperial pound was defined in law in 1824 it was set as 7,000 grains. However, as imperial measures became official British measurements the older customary weights began to fade from use. Pharmacists nevertheless continued to dispense medicines in grains (based on the apothecaries' system) until the 1970s, when metric measurements were finally brought in. Although grains have fallen out of common usage in modern Britain, they are still used for the measurement of bullets, bullet casings and arrows. For more on the grain (or barleycorn) as a unit of length, see page 48.

Dram

Today a dram has come to mean colloquially a small amount of anything, but it is most often used to denote a small measure of liquid. Traditionally, however, a dram was an actual British unit of weight. Somewhat confusingly it came to have two different weights, one under the apothecaries' system (used by pharmacists) and another under the avoirdupois system (used for trade measurements before metrification). These two systems were developed by different sectors, which would use their measures in a particular context. This meant that both systems took the traditional dram as a measure, but the actual weight and usage differed. In the apothecaries' system the dram is made up of 3 scruples (see page 106), which are themselves 20 grains (see page 16) each – this puts the apothecaries' dram at 60 grains, which is ⅛ of an apothecaries' ounce (480 grains). For apothecaries mixing tiny amounts of powders and liquids to make up medicines, the dram was a relatively large measure. The avoirdupois dram, however, is the smallest measure in that system, being equivalent to one-sixteenth of an avoirdupois ounce (437½ grains). The apothecaries' dram (60 grains) is therefore significantly larger than the avoirdupois dram (approximately 27 grains). In 1900 the British government attempted to differentiate between the two drams by officially modifying the spelling so the apothecaries' dram became the drachm. This modified spelling recalls the origin of the word 'dram', which can be traced back to the Ancient Greek coin the drachma. This silver coin was introduced in around 500 BCE, its name deriving from the Greek verb meaning 'to grasp' and relating to the handful of 6 obols (the smallest Greek coin) which made up the value of one drachma. As the main unit of currency for the Hellenic world, the word 'drachma' spread to the Roman Empire as the Latinized *dragma* and from there into Old French (*dragme*) and Middle English (*dragme*), and was adopted to describe the weight of something equivalent to the coin. Over time the word in English morphed into 'dram' and came to be described as a small measure of anything. The dram, although rarely referred to in common usage today, remains the smallest weight in the avoirdupois system, with 16 drams making up 1 ounce.

In England dram also came to be a measurement of volume and meant a small amount of cordial or alcohol. Dram shops selling small quantities of spirits such as brandy or gin became popular in the eighteenth century. In Scotland drams became associated with whisky, and the measurement, although never officially given an exact volume, was taken to mean the amount you can swallow in one mouthful.

The volume of a dram is officially taken to be ⅛ of a fluid ounce, which translates to roughly 3.6 ml. This tiny amount is more like a sip than a mouthful, so in order to avoid disappointment it is necessary to differentiate between the official liquid dram and the whisky dram when ordering a measure of your favourite malt. In the UK the standard single measure for a whisky is either 25 ml (which is classed as 1 unit of alcohol) or 35 ml, so it could be argued that this is the measure for a dram of whisky. However, the beauty of a hand-poured wee dram is that it is undefined, so you can slosh in as much or as little into your glass as befits your mood.

Pennyweight

The pennyweight is an old British customary measure – larger than a grain but less than an ounce. It developed because an English penny was originally a unit of both weight and monetary value. Up until decimalization the penny was represented by the letter *d*, which was short for *denarius* – the Roman coin upon which it was based. For this reason the pennyweight was abbreviated to 'dwt'. King Offa of Mercia introduced the first 'modern' pennies in about 775 CE. Their value was pegged to their weight and they were ¹⁄₂₄₀ of a Saxon pound of silver (which is about 5,400 grains or *c.* 350 grams). Later, in the Middle Ages, the pennyweight was pegged to the Tower pound of 7,680 Tower grains and defined as ¹⁄₂₀ of an ounce. In 1527 troy weights replaced Tower weights, so the pennyweight was now defined against the troy pound of 5,760 grains. This made the pennyweight 24 grains or ¹⁄₂₀ of a troy ounce. The troy units of measure – grain, pennyweight, ounce and pound – came to be used largely for coins, precious metals or jewellery and remained in use until 1878 when the Weights and Measures Act took away their official status. Only the troy ounce was still allowed to be used and then only in the context of precious metals. The pennyweight is still used unofficially by some jewellery makers when measuring precious metals, and also by some dentists, who use pennyweights when calculating how much metal to use in a filling or crown. Today the value of pennies is no longer tied to their weight, so the use of precious metals in coinage has waned. This means that coins no longer hold any intrinsic value.

Pounds & ounces

The pound of weight originates in the Roman Empire, where it was known as *libra pondo*. It derived from the Latin word *libra*, which like the sign of the zodiac meant a balance or scale but was also used to refer to a measure – pound by weight. This Latin word is the reason why pounds are abbreviated as lb – a shortening of the word *libra*. Initially coins made from precious metals were also used as a weight measurement, linking coins to weight. This explains why the symbol for the British pound sterling (£) derives from the *L* of *libra* with a line through it to show it is an abbreviation (for more on this see my *Hyphens & Hashtags*). Incidentally, the old Italian currency the lira also derives its name and symbol from the Latin *libra*. Ounce comes from the Latin word *uncia*, meaning one-twelfth part, which was used in the Roman world to refer to an ounce and also to an inch. It came to be used in English by the early fourteenth century from the Old French *unce*, and it was defined as ¹⁄₁₂ of a troy pound.

The Romans brought the pound weight to Britain, where it was originally used to weigh amounts in gold or silver, and later came to be used by merchants in trade. Unfortunately a number of different pounds diverged from the original Roman pound as they came to be used in different contexts. In Britain alone there was the troy pound, the apothecaries' pound, the Tower pound and the mercantile pound. The troy pound is thought to be named after the French mercantile city of Troyes, which played host to an important medieval fair where a great deal of trading took place. It is based on the grain as the smallest unit of weight, with 5,760 grains (or 24 grains in a pennyweight, 20 pennyweight in an ounce and 12 ounces in a pound) making up a pound. Troy weight was used from the Middle Ages as the main method of measuring small amounts of precious metals and stones; it is one of the oldest weighing systems used in Britain. The apothecaries' pound weighed the same as the troy pound and used the same measure of 12 ounces to the pound, but where it differed was in the smaller measures that made up the pound. This is because apothecaries' measures were used by pharmacists to mix their medicines, and so the system needed to include some very small amounts. The grain was still the smallest measure but this went into a scruple (which was 20 grains), then a drachm (which was 3 scruples), and 8 drachms made an ounce. The Tower pound was created after William the Conqueror invaded Britain in 1066. While he allowed the natives to retain their systems of measurement, he decreed that the standards (the example weights against which all others must be tested) be moved from Winchester to the Tower of London. The Tower pound was used purely for the minting of coins and was made up of 5,400 grains or 15 ounces. The troy, apothecaries' and Tower pound all had their own specific uses in Britain, but for most other measurements the mercantile pound was used, which came in at 6,750 grains or 15 ounces.

By the fourteenth century both the Tower pound and the mercantile pound were based on different measurements of 15 ounces, with the Tower pound coming out lighter. This confusing state of affairs was sometimes exploited by merchants, who would choose to use the lighter Tower pound to their advantage. Later, the dominance of the English wool trade saw more and more merchants adopting the European avoirdupois pound of 16 ounces. English wool merchants mostly traded with weavers and dyers from the Continent, who favoured the avoirdupois system as it was easily divisible into three even numbers – half, half and half again. As a result by the

Tudor period, Henry VII (r. 1485–1509) had made the avoirdupois pound standard, which caused the mercantile pound of 15 ounces to become obsolete. Elizabeth I also decreed that the avoirdupois system should be standard. In an effort to avoid confusion with the various competing pounds, in 1588 she set the English (avoirdupois) imperial pound at 7,000 troy grains. This remained the standard measure for a pound until 1959, when all the countries using this measure (USA, UK, Canada, Australia, New Zealand and South Africa) reached an international agreement to standardize pounds and ounces based on a metric measure. The international pound was agreed to be equivalent to 0.45359237 kilograms, which is approximately 6 ten-millionths of a kilogram lighter than the imperial pound.

The troy pound remained in use for precious metals until 1878, when it was abolished (although the troy ounce was retained for measuring gems and bullion). By the time it too was abolished in 1978, the apothecaries' pound had long been out of use. Today the pound is no longer 'officially' used in Britain, having been replaced by metric measurements. However, such was its widespread customary use that the pound is still seen in some contexts. For example, anyone overeating might tell people they have been 'piling on the pounds', and when babies are born their weight is often still given in pounds and ounces. In 1973 when Britain joined the EU it became a requirement for the nation to switch to the French metric system in order to integrate with their European trading partners. There was a great deal of resistance to this change and so it was decided to take a gradual approach. To aid this slow shift, in 1985 it was ruled that imperial and metric measures had parity. But the pressure to conform to European standards continued and in 1994 new regulations required measurements to be given in metric. Market traders continued to oppose the changes, and in 2001 several 'metric martyrs' were convicted of selling goods solely in imperial measures. Ultimately in 2008 the EU recognized the futility of trying to do away completely with traditional British imperial measures and ruled that measurements such as pints, miles and pounds could be used alongside their metric equivalents. British weighing scales and recipe books continue to use both kilograms and pounds and ounces, but schoolchildren today are taught solely in metric, creating something of a generational divide.

Kilogram

In 1793 the French grasped the nettle and decided to introduce the metric system: a method of defining standard weights and measures based on natural laws. Scientists had been calling for such a system for many years, as the huge variety of local weights and measures used across France meant that they were open to exploitation. It was common for peasants to work a customary amount decreed by their landlord; for example, they might be required to weed an ell of land, but as an ell was not standardized landowners could stretch their ells to get extra work out of their tenants. It was similarly difficult for the government trying to collect taxes. With a huge variety of local customary measures coexisting, it was nigh on impossible to gain reliable figures on the amount of each goods an area was producing, making taxation difficult to calculate. The metric system was designed to correct this issue by introducing standard measures that were based on immutable natural laws.

The kilogram was based on the *grave*, which had been proposed in the early 1700s and related to the weight of 1 litre of water at just above freezing. To establish its exact weight the measurement took place in a vacuum. However, this was not entirely accurate as air pressure affects mass. The concept of the kilogram, made up of 1,000 grams, however was set. In 1799 a platinum kilogram was built which was to serve as the standard kilogram by which all others would be measured, and it was lodged in the French archives. France embraced the new metric system and many other countries followed suit, seeing the benefit of these standardized weights and measures, not least for their ability to create a solid foundation for science and technology. As with any innovation the metric system took a while to be accepted, but by 1875 seventeen nations (Argentina, Austria-Hungary, Belgium, Brazil, Denmark, France, Germany, Italy, Peru, Portugal, Russia, Spain, Sweden and Norway, Switzerland, the Ottoman Empire, the United States of America, and Venezuela) met in France to sign the Treaty of the Metre. This established the International Bureau of Weights and Measures (BIPM), which was to coordinate international metrology. One of the innovations of this conference was the creation in 1889 of a superior version of the kilogram, crafted from platinum and iridium.

The metal cylinder, known as the International Prototype Kilogram (IPK), or more colloquially as *Le Grand K*, was kept under a series of glass bell jars to preserve it and stashed safely in a laboratory in Sèvres. This platinum–iridium kilogram was the world's one true kilogram, to which all others would be compared. The IPK remained the type specimen of the kilogram until 1989, when a regular weighing session indicated, to the horror of metrologists around the world, that the IPK was now some 50 micrograms lighter than its replicas kept in various locations across the globe. The reasons for this anomaly were unknown, but some speculated that overenthusiastic cleaning might have caused the degradation of the IPK, or that perhaps the copies had simply absorbed dust and thus mass over the years. Whatever the cause, metrologists agreed that this was an unacceptable state of affairs for such a key piece of scientific equipment. As a result it became apparent that a new, more reliable way of defining the kilogram was needed. This was no small feat and it took many years and many brains to come up with an adequate solution. But finally in 2018 it was announced that *Le Grand K* would be retired and that henceforth the kilogram would be defined not from a physical artefact but in relation to fundamental constants in natural law. The constant chosen was the Planck Constant, which essentially meant that the weight of a kilogram would be defined using electric current and voltage. This new definition means that, provided it has the right equipment, any laboratory in the world can ascertain an exact kilogram. The kilogram was the final metric measurement to retain a physical example of its weight, but now it too is defined by the natural laws of the universe.

Bushel & peck

Most people today might be familiar with the word 'bushel' through the biblical idiom 'Hiding your light under a bushel' (Matthew 5:15). The phrase relates to an oil lamp being hidden under a container (rendering it invisible), and means that you should not hide your talents. This implies that the measure 'bushel' was ancient, but actually this phrasing was introduced into the Bible by William Tyndale in the sixteenth century when he produced a new translation of the New Testament. The bushel used by Tyndale is another word for bowl. The bushel as a measure was of Anglo-Saxon origin. It was used to measure commodities such as wheat, wine, beans and grain, and could be applied to both dry goods and liquid measures. The bushel was used as a midway weight between the pound and a ton, and comprised 4 pecks or 8 gallons. During the reign of Edgar the Peaceful (959–975 CE) it was decreed that standards of all the key weights and measures should be kept in Winchester and London. As a result the bushel and its parts – pecks, gallons, quarts and pints – became known as the 'Winchester Measure'. The Winchester Measure was defined as the volume of a cylinder 18.5 inches in diameter and 8 inches deep, and this was used as the standard for measuring agricultural goods across England until superseded by the Imperial Measure in 1824. The word 'bushel' likely derives from the Old French *boissel*, which probably comes from the French grain measure *boisse*, which was itself named from the Gallo-Roman *bostia,* meaning 'handful'. Despite the existence of the Winchester Measure a number of different bushels were used, often weighing different amounts depending on the commodity weighed. The Imperial Measure was introduced in 1824 in an attempt to rectify the disarray and was set at 80 avoirdupois pounds or 8 imperial gallons. Despite this new standard, in 1862 a Parliamentary Select Committee Report into weights and measures discov-ered that over twenty different bushel measurements were being used across England, indicating that it was still a popular customary measure. The move to metrification in the 1960s finally signalled the end of bushels and pecks in Britain, as they were officially abolished from 1 January 1969. However, echoes of their former widespread use remain in popular songs and rhymes such as 'Peter Piper', who picked a peck of pickled peppers.

In America both bushels and pecks continue to be used although their amounts vary, depending on the item to be weighed. Unlike in Britain, where bushels and pecks were used to measure both dry weights and the volume of wet goods, in America bushels were only used for dry goods. Traditionally the American bushel is based on the old Winchester Measure and is used for agricultural goods. To try to standardize the bushel, each state was sent an exact standard bushel to work from. However, some states measured their bushels 'struck', which means level, whereas others used a 'heaped' measure. This confusion has persisted, and in American commodity markets each grain is assigned its own standard weight, which is then measured in bushels. For example, a bushel of oats is set at 32 lb whereas a bushel of wheat is 60 lb. This variance means that the bushel is mainly used only in commodity markets and retains little meaning to ordinary Americans.

Stone

The beauty of the stone as a unit of measure was that any locality could identify a rock of decent dimensions and adopt it as the local stone in weight. Since antiquity a stone had been used as a measure, although it did not need to be assigned an actual value. Instead, any good-sized stone could be used as a counterbalance to ensure that commodities could be equally split, meaning that this system could be used in societies where arithmetic had yet to develop. Across northern Europe stones were used in this way to measure dry goods, with the earliest examples dating back to the Roman Empire. There was little standardization, and the weight of stones could vary from country to country, region to region and even village to village, ranging from as little as 4 lb all the way up to 40 lb. It was not only the location which affected the weight of the stone; sometimes the weight varied depending on the goods being weighed. For example, an English statute from *c.* 1300 set a London stone at 12.5 lb; however, a stone for weighing lead was said to be 12 lb, while a stone for measuring beeswax, sugar, pepper, cumin, almonds and alum was 8 lb, and the stone for weighing glass was 5 lb. The inconsistent and archaic use of stones continued in Britain for some time. An example of this can be seen in the system used by British butchers: the stone used for measuring the weight of livestock was generally accepted to be 14 lb but the resultant meat was measured with an 8 lb stone. It is thought that this was because butchers would return the dressed meat from an animal carcass back to the farmer stone for stone – the weight difference meant that the butcher could keep the blood, offal and hide as payment. Butchers at Smithfield Meat Market in London continued to employ the 8 lb stone right up until World War II.

As the wool trade became increasingly important to Britain the wool stone was in 1350 set by statute at 14 lb, although different stones were still permitted for use for other commodities. A variety of different stones depending on the commodity being traded continued to coexist for hundreds of years until 1835, when it was decided that an overarching imperial stone should be codified. Perhaps because wool had been such a key commodity in England the wool stone of 14 lb was selected to become the imperial stone. Scotland largely used a stone based on 16 Scottish pounds until 1824, when an act made all weights and measures uniform across the United Kingdom. Despite the introduction of the imperial stone, a parliamentary committee reported in 1862 on the confusion of the current state of weights and measures in Britain, stating that fourteen different stone weights were currently in use. By the 1970s Britain's increasingly close trading relationship with the European Union meant that most businesses were keen for Britain to adopt metric measures. The stone fell out of favour for trade, although it was still permitted to be used as a 'supplementary unit', which meant it could be used as long as metric measures were given alongside it. But by 1985 the stone was officially removed from the list of measurements that could be legally used for trade purposes. Despite metrification, many Britons continue to give their weight, or the weight of their livestock, in stones and pounds. An interesting side note is that, although the stone was not greatly used in America, in 1790 Thomas Jefferson suggested a new decimal system of coinage, weights and measures. His decimal currency was adopted, but his idea to introduce an American stone of 10 lb (with each pound weighing 10 ounces) was rejected.

Hundredweight

Today in Britain the hundredweight would be defined as 8 stone or 112 pounds or 1,792 ounces, meaning it is not one hundred of anything. So why the name? Before 1350 the hundredweight was used to measure large amounts of goods and was generally defined as 100 pounds, hence the name. However, in 1350 King Edward III changed the value of the stone used for weighing wool from 12.5 pounds to 14 pounds. This was to have far-reaching effects, not least on the hundredweight, which was still based on 8 stone. A stone was now 14 lb, which meant that the new hundredweight became 112 lb.

This hundredweight became part of the British imperial system and was commonly used until the twentieth century, with 20 hundredweight making 1 ton. America, however, chose to use the traditional (and more sensible) 100 lb avoirdupois hundredweight. This caused some difficulty with British merchants importing tobacco and wheat from America. The American hundredweight (also known as the short hundredweight in Britain) was banned from use by the British government in the 1824 Weights and Measures Act due to concerns about fraud. However, in 1879 the British government agreed to allow the measure to be used for trade with America as long as it was called a 'cental' (ctl) in order to differentiate it from the imperial hundredweight (cwt).

With metrification in Britain the hundredweight became an outmoded unit of weight, and similarly it is rarely used in America today except for livestock and some cereals. Traces of the old hundredweight measure can be found stamped on old anvils. These huge and heavy bits of metalworking equipment used by blacksmiths were traditionally stamped with a three-digit number that revealed their weight. The first figure shows the anvil's weight in hundredweight (112 lb), the second is in quarter-hundredweights (28 lb) and the final number is whole pounds. If an anvil was stamped with 2.1.5, for example, then in total it would weigh $2 \times 112 + 1 \times 28 + 5 = 257$ lb.

Ton & tonne

The ton is the largest measure of weight, but it derives from a measure of volume. The word 'ton' comes from 'tun', the biggest cask used to store and transport wine (see page 118). Charmingly this word came from the French *tonnerre*, which means thunder, because this was reminiscent of the rumbling noise produced as the huge casks of wine were rolled along. Tons are especially confusing because the British and American ton differ from each other and from the divergently spelled (but identically pronounced) metric tonne. Not only do these three tons differ in weight but, to muddy the waters, there are also numerous other niche tons used in shipping and industry. Let's start with the British ton, which as already mentioned derives from the largest type of wine cask, the tun, which held roughly 252 wine gallons. This huge cask came to visually represent anything that weighed a lot, and so the concept of the ton as a unit of weight developed. By the thirteenth century the British ton became standardized as one of the traditional units of measurement, so it was officially based on 20 hundredweight (cwt) (see page 38). Each hundredweight weighs 8 stone and each stone weighs 14 pounds, so in Britain the ton weighed 20 × 8 × 14 = 2,240 pounds. This ton was used to measure bulk items and so it came to be known as the 'long ton' to differentiate it from the smaller American ton, which became known as the 'short ton'. The British ton was also known as the imperial ton as it was part of the imperial system. However, since the 1985 Weights and Measures Act the imperial ton has been outlawed and replaced by the metric ton.

The American short ton is also made up of 20 hundredweight, but in America a hundredweight is 100 pounds. As a result the American short ton is 2,000 pounds. The metric ton, known as a tonne, but pronounced the same as ton, is 1,000 kilograms, which is 2,204.6 pounds, and this is used across the world. In SI Units (the modern International System of Units for the metric system) the tonne goes by the rather jazzier name: megagram. In shipping a ton is used to describe a variety of different weights. The register ton (also known as tonnage) is a volume measurement of the capacity of a ship, whereas the displacement ton is the actual weight of a ship, which is calculated by working out how much water the ship displaces and then converting that volume into weight. The deadweight ton (dwt) reveals the ship's carrying capacity in terms of overall weight, so it takes account of not just cargo but also ballast and crew. Colloquially in Britain a 'ton' is used to mean 100 of anything, so someone speeding on the motorway might be said to have been 'doing a ton'. The profusion of different weights and definitions ascribed to the word 'ton' has caused much confusion over the years, a situation perfectly exemplified by the unfortunate story of NASA's Mars Climate Orbiter. In 1999 the Orbiter approaching Mars burnt up in its atmosphere, scattering debris across the planet's surface. This was because the engineers making the Orbiter used imperial tons to calculate the force the thrusters needed to exert, whereas the software used to deploy the thrusters used metric measurements. This ton-related error resulted in the unmanned Orbiter's catastrophic loss.

Wool weight

Wool was the most important British commodity from the twelfth to the nineteenth century. In 1607 antiquarian William Camden described wool as 'one of the pillars of the State', reflecting its crucial role in the British economy. The climate was thought to produce the finest wool in the world; across the nation sheep were farmed and numerous people were employed in processing, packing and transporting wool to the Continent. Initially most raw wool was traded to France, but by the fourteenth century war with France had caused merchants to switch to trading with Flanders, where numerous skilled spinners and weavers lived and worked. By the sixteenth century political and religious unrest began affecting Flanders and so Flemish weavers were encouraged to move to England and train up local workers.

This meant that by the mid-sixteenth century an increased amount of English wool was now being spun into cloth domestically and then imported to the Netherlands, Italy, Poland and Germany.

Due to the success of the wool trade, English monarchs began to tax wool heavily, meaning that it became increasingly important that the volume of wool traded could be accurately measured. In 1497 Henry VII issued a series of shield-shaped weights made from bronze and embossed with the king's coat of arms. These were issued to the 'tronators' who were employed to ride across England to the many wool fairs weighing the local 'wool clip' (the total yield of shorn wool for one season) for tax purposes. These weights came in pairs of 7 lb, 14 lb or 28 lb avoirdupois. A leather thong was slotted through a hole in the weights, which allowed them to be slung over the saddle like a saddlebag to prevent the horse from becoming unbalanced by badly distributed weights. When weighing the wool clip the leather thong was thrown over a beam and the weight was used to counterbalance the sack of wool to be weighed. Naturally the wool trade produced its own language to refer to the various wool weights. The smallest weight of 7 lb was known as a clove (the clove was also used to weigh butter or cheese, but in that context it was 8 lb) and 2 cloves made a stone of 14 lb. Two stones made a tod of 28 lb. The word 'tod' is thought to come from Old Icelandic *toddi*, meaning 'bit' or 'piece'. Actual physical wool weights as used by tronators came in cloves, stones and tods, but further conceptual weight names were used for larger amounts; for example, 6½ tods made a wey (182 lb), and 2 weys made a sack (364 lb or 26 stone). Some fifteenth-century texts explained that the wool sack had 364 lb due to the Roman system of measurement which saw 1 lb of wool added to a sack every day of the year except one. To accentuate the importance of the wool trade to the British economy since the reign of King Edward III (r. 1327–77) the Lord Chancellor of England has sat on a wool sack covered in red cloth. In 1938 the 'Woolsack' in the House of Lords had become a bit threadbare so it was decided it should be refurbished. When the sack was dismantled it was shockingly discovered to have been stuffed with horsehair rather than the traditional wool. A new Woolsack was then recreated with wool sourced from around the Commonwealth to symbolize unity. Since 2006, when constitutional reform split the role of the Lord Speaker from the role of the Lord Chancellor, the Woolsack is now the seat of the Lord Speaker of the House of Lords.

Today wool for export is weighed in kilograms. The wool is usually packed into bales which are compressed mechanically by a wool press and have a standard minimum weight of 120 kg (265 lb).

COMBMARTIN.

TO BE SOLD

BY AUCTION,

At the KING'S ARMS INN in Combmartin,

On Wednesday the Fifth Day of January next, at the Hour of
Three o'Clock in the Afternoon,

The FEE-SIMPLE and INHERITANCE of the undermentioned

MESSUAGES,

TENEMENTS, and LANDS,

Situate in the Parish of COMBMARTIN:

LOT 1.---A new erected Dwelling House and Outhouses, Orchard
and Garden, and two Closes of Rich Meadow Land adjoining,
called SPURWAYS, containing about 2 Acres 2 Roods, now
in the occupation of George Knight.

LOT 2.---A Dwelling House, Barn, Outhouses, and Garden, and a
Close of Rich Meadow Land adjoining, called LUCAS'S,
containing about 3 Roods.

LOT 3.---Two Closes of Rich Meadow Land called the LADDER
PARKS, containing about 3 Acres 11 Perches.

LOT 4.---A Close of Rich Meadow Land called WEBBER'S
DEAN, containing about 1 Acre 11 Perches.

LOT 5.---A Close of Rich Meadow Land called THORNE'S
DEAN, containing about 1 Acre 1 Rood.

LOT 6.---A Close of Meadow Land called SHAMBLE'S HAY,
containing about 2 Acres 4 Perches.

LOT 7.---A small Close of Meadow Land called LUCAS'S, containing about 2 Roods.

For viewing the Premises apply at the King's Arms in Combmartin, and for further
Particulars to Mr. CHARLES ROBERTS, Solicitor, Barnstaple.

Dated 29th November, 1819,

SYLE, Printer, Barnstaple.

LENGTH & AREA

'The wonder is, not that the field of the stars
is so vast, but that man has measured it.'

ANATOLE FRANCE

Barleycorn

The barleycorn is one of the smallest ancient measures of length. Unlike most early measures, which were based on parts of the human body, this one was based on another widespread and accessible item – a grain of cereal. The story begins in about 8000 BCE in what is known as the Fertile Crescent (modern-day Jordan, Iraq, Egypt, Israel and Syria), where the earliest archaeological evidence for the domestication of barley has been identified. By around 4000 BCE the climate in Britain had warmed sufficiently to allow Neolithic people in the south to begin to clear forest and plant crops. Barley and wheat seeds both arrived via trade routes from the Middle East; by the time of the Roman invasion in 43 CE barley was a staple crop in Britain. Unlike wild barley, cultivated barley had a much more regular shape. As a result hulled barley taken from the centre of an ear had a relatively standard size and so when it was laid end to end it could provide a relatively accurate measure. Barleycorns had been used as a form of measurement in this way in a number of early civilizations. For example, in the region of Syria, Jordan and Iraq the width of a horse or camel hair was used as the smallest measurement. Six camel hairs were said to be equivalent to one barleycorn, and six barleycorn

made up one *assbaa*, or finger. It seems likely that as the grain was traded up from the Middle East so too was the measurement it was used to represent.

References to barleycorns as a unit of measurement are seen in a number of early medieval texts; for example, in the Welsh Venedotian Code of Dyvnwal, which defined land area in Gwynedd with the barleycorn as its smallest measure. By the fourteenth century the barleycorn was used across Britain, but its relationship to larger units of length differed, causing consternation and confusion for traders. The Welsh foot was customarily 27 barleycorns, whereas the Saxon foot was considered 39 barleycorns. Edward II (r. 1307–27) decided the matter needed to be settled, and so in 1324 he issued a decree: 'Three barley-corns, round and dry, make an inch.' This pronouncement clarified that there were 36 barleycorns in an English foot. The barleycorn remained the smallest customary measure of length in Britain (although fractions of an inch were more frequently used to describe small sizes) until metrification brought in the millimetre.

Some remnant of the barleycorn persists in Britain today, surviving in UK shoe sizes. Originally most ordinary people hand-fashioned their shoes at home so official shoe sizes were not necessary. For the wealthy, a professional shoemaker would be employed and they would make a template of their customer's foot, known as a last. This meant that shoes were made to fit an individual's foot and so they did not need to be given a unit of measurement. As a result, standardization in shoe sizes came rather late. It is not until 1856 that the first documentary evidence for the use of barleycorns as increments in shoe sizes is found in Britain. This is in Robert Gardiner's *The Illustrated Handbook of the Foot*. Despite this late appearance in print it is likely that shoemakers had customarily used the barleycorn in sizing for hundreds of years before that. Children's sizes started at size zero, which was set at 4 inches (12 barleycorns). This was said to be the width of a man's hand and the average size of a child's foot as they began walking. Children's shoe sizes went up to size 13, with adult sizes starting at size 1 and going up to a size 12. Each full size went up in increments of one barleycorn. In 1880 American Edwin B. Simpson invented a more accurate foot-measuring system which incorporated the width of the foot, and he also suggested the use of half-sizes to improve fit. Thereafter American shoe sizes diverged slightly from British but they still maintained the unit of one barleycorn between each full size, ensuring that this small cereal-based measure quietly lives on.

Inch

An inch is defined as ¹⁄₁₂ of a foot or ¹⁄₃₆ of a yard. Its relationship to the number twelve is where we get its name from. In Old English it was known as *ynce*, which comes from the Latin *uncia*, meaning one-twelfth. This explains its relationship to the Roman measurement of a foot. Incidentally the Latin *uncia* is also the root of the word ounce (see page 24). An inch was widely accepted to be a small length, but its exact definition was debated. The first written record of an inch in England is in an early-seventh-century text known as Æthelberht's Code, which survives only in a copy of *c.* 1120 preserved at Rochester Cathedral, known as *Textus Roffensis*. The Code lays out Old English laws and records the penalties for various 'crimes'. In one passage the Code discusses the penalties for stabbing someone in the thigh, specifying that the aggressor must pay 6 shillings for each 'thrust' and a further shilling if the wound is over an inch; two shillings for a wound of 2 inches; and three shillings for anything over 3 inches. This fascinating insight into Anglo-Saxon culture does not specify the dimension of the inch, which suggests that it was likely a commonly understood measurement.

In England the inch was customarily described as the length of three barleycorns, and this was codified during the reign of King Edward II (1307–27) when it was decreed that an inch was equivalent to three grains of barley, placed end to end lengthwise (see page 49). An inch was also sometimes based on placing twelve poppy seeds end to end. In other parts of Europe, however, the customary inch was more often described as the length of a man's thumb. This difference is reflected in the local names given to the inch across Europe, including in French *pouce*, Swedish *tum*, Dutch *duim* and Czech *palec*, all of which come from the word 'thumb'. In around 1150 the Scottish king David I defined an inch as the breadth of a man's thumb at the base of the nail. It was recommended that a small man's thumb, a medium-sized man's thumb and a large man's thumb were all measured, added together and then divided by three to achieve the most accurate inch.

Up until the nineteenth century in Britain an inch continued to be defined as 3 barleycorns, but as scientific method became increasingly important a number of scholars began to question the continuing accuracy of this unit of measure. A barleycorn, it was recognized, was rarely standard in length. For hundreds of years, however, an official metal standard inch had been preserved at the Exchequer, which had been created based on three barleycorns and was now itself the standard. This made the standard inch somewhat arbitrary. To try to improve accuracy, in 1824 the inch was instead defined against the imperial standard yard. However, this still meant the measure was taken from a physical metal bar representing the standard.

The Americans had initially used the British standards to define their inch but in 1866 they decided greater accuracy would be obtained if they defined the inch in relation to the metre, even though they had not adopted metric measures. As a result 1 metre was codified as equal to 39.37 inches. This was further clarified in 1893 when the Mendenhall Order was passed, which required all American customary units to be based on the international prototype metre, rather than British imperial standards. Metre bars numbered 21 and 27 which the Americans had received from the General Conference on Weights and Measures were deemed most accurate, and so it was from these new metal standards that the American inch measure was taken. This change saw the US and the British inch diverge, with the US inch classified as 25.4000508 mm whereas the British inch was fractionally smaller at 25.399977 mm.

For industry and international trade the fractional difference in the British and American inch became problematic. To try to get round this, in 1930 the British Standards Institution (BSI) officially created an 'industrial inch' of 25.4 mm. The reasoning behind this change likely came from the Swedish inventor Carl Edvard Johansson, who in 1912 had begun producing metal gauge blocks in inch sizes for precision measuring. Johansson decided to split the difference between the American and English inches and began manufacturing inch gauge blocks that were a standard 25.4 mm. Johansson's inch blocks were so popular that other manufacturers followed his lead and soon the 25.4 mm inch was standard across across all sectors internationally. The American Standards Association also adopted an inch of 25.4 mm in 1933 and it soon became the standard internationally. Today in Britain the inch is largely superseded by metric measurements but it lurks on in a number of measures. Heights are still frequently given in feet and inches, and it is still common for television, tablet and mobile phone screen sizes to be given in inches.

Hand

The hand has long been used as a simple tool for measurement, but in Britain today it has become associated solely with measuring horses. In Ancient Egypt the standard measure of a cubit was divided into seven palms, a palm being roughly 3.7 inches. The palm was widely used across the ancient world; it was generally considered to be the width of a man's hand, including the thumb. In England several terms and measures relating to the hand were used interchangeably – the palm, fist or handbreadth – and they were all around 3 inches in length, although some included the thumb and others used a clenched fist. The measure slowly fell out of fashion as it was superseded in most contexts by other measures such as the inch, the foot or the yard. However, the hand remained the standard for measuring equines. It is not known for certain why horses have historically been measured in hands, but it is likely that it was because it is a simple way to assess a horse's height in the field by laying your flattened palm one above the other. A horse's height is a key aspect of its value, with larger horses generally fetching higher prices. As a result it became important to have an accepted standard for this measure. So in 1540 Henry VIII officially decreed that a hand was equal to 4 inches.

A horse should be standing on a flat surface when it is measured. Horses are measured from the ground to the highest point on their back, known as the withers. The withers are the knobbly part found at the base of a horse's neck. Unlike a horse's head, which is liable to bob up and down, making it unsuitable as a base measure, the withers are stable. Most people use a measuring stick which has measurements notched down the side and a sliding horizontal bar. The stick is placed next to the horse's front legs and the horizontal bar is moved down the stick until it rests on the withers, giving the horse's height. Hands are not fractional, so measurements are given in whole hands and inches. For example, a horse measuring 62 inches would be said to be 15 hands and 2 inches, given as 15.2 hh. Hands are used to measure horses not just in Britain but in much of the English-speaking world such as the United States, Australia and Canada. In the United Kingdom the measuring of horses is overseen by the Joint Measurement Board (JMB). For official measures they require the horse to be over the age of four years and to be measured without horseshoes on.

Foot

The average foot of a man makes an obvious unit of rough measurement, and so it was that this measure was widely used in antiquity across the Roman and Greek empires (whereas in Egypt and the Middle East the cubit, or forearm length, was more commonly used; see page 61). Naturally, using a body part to measure distance or length led to a great deal of variance in the actual size of the measure, often depending on the height of the person proffering their foot. The foot was most commonly divided into 12 inches or 16 digits. In 1647 the mathematician John Greaves travelled to Rome and measured a number of Roman monuments, statues and extant measuring rods, and concluded that the Roman foot, also known as the *pes*, was 294.86 mm. In Ancient Greece the foot was said to be ⅟₆₀₀ of a *stadion* (181.2 metres), which would make a Greek foot 302 mm. Regional variations aside, the foot as a unit of measure came to be widely used across Europe. In 790 CE Charlemagne tried to standardize the foot across the Frankish kingdom. He decreed that the Frankish foot (known as *pied*) should be set at ⅙ of a *toise*, which is the span of an average man with his arms outstretched; in modern terms this set the Frankish foot at *c.* 326.6 mm. Recent analysis of buildings built across Charlemagne's kingdom during his reign, however, show a number of different values for the foot, from 296 mm to 340 mm, indicating that his decree did not translate into common practice.

In Britain, archaeologists have suggested the existence of a Neolithic long foot, evidence for which they have taken from measurements at Stonehenge, Durrington Walls and Folkton Drums, among others. The Neolithic long foot was proposed to have been 12.672 inches. In Wales a foot of 9 inches was said to have been decreed by legendary Welsh king Dyfnwal Moelmud. With the Roman conquest of Britain in 43 CE, Roman units of measurement, including the foot, became the dominant method of measurement, although the Belgic foot of 13.2 inches was also used for land measurements. From around 950 CE an iron yardstick held at Winchester was used as the standard basis for a foot in England. The foot was further codified by a statute between 1266 and 1303 known as the Composition of Yards and Perches (BL Cotton MS Claudius D ii). This document set out standard English measurements in relation to one another with the barleycorn as its basis:

> 3 grains of barley dry and round do make an inch, 12 inches make 1 foot, 3 feet make 1 yard, 5 yards and a half make a perch, and 40 perches in length and 4 in breadth make an acre.

Codifications such as these confirmed the foot as 12 inches. Although the exact length could still vary, the base of 12 remained.

In America the newly independent colonies initially kept customary British measures. In 1790 George Washington reiterated the national importance of establishing a standard system of weights and measures. In 1815 a brass yard bar made by London instrument maker Edward Troughton arrived in America to form the basis of their measurement system, and it was from this standard that copies were made and sent out to each state. However, by 1866 the arbitrary British yard, feet and inches began to seem unscientific and so Congress decided that American measurements should be based on the metre. The Mendenhall Order of 1893 saw metric measurements adopted across America, which meant that the foot became a fraction of a metre. Unfortunately the maths didn't quite work and so the foot ended up being an ungainly run-on of decimal places starting 0.3048006096... To fix this unhappy problem the American government decided in 1959 to adopt instead the international foot of 0.3048 of a metre.

The international foot had been suggested in 1953 by the international community after microscope technology had greatly improved, meaning that national differences in standard feet had become ever more noticeable. The international foot was agreed as 0.3048 metres, based on the international yard of 0.9144 metres. It was adopted by the USA, Canada and the Commonwealth nations, and in 1963 the UK also agreed to use the international foot as standard. Now that America had adopted the international foot it had a neater relationship to the metre but it created a new problem: the new foot differed by two parts per million from the old foot. Wedded to the old ways, map-makers from the US National Survey were granted permission to continue to use the old 1893 foot and this became known as the US survey foot. The difference between the two feet is not noticeable to the naked eye, but over vast distances it begins to tell, making 2 feet of difference for every 1 million feet. These two marginally different feet have coexisted in America for over sixty years, but this has now come to an end. The National Institute of Standards and Technology has decreed that having these two different feet is contrary to the intent of uniform standards, and so as of 1 January 2023 the US survey foot became obsolete and the international foot became the only foot in use in America. To try to reduce disruption and confusion the international foot will become known as 'the foot', indicating to everyone that from then on there is just one type of foot in all America.

Cubit

The etymology of the English word 'cubit' reveals that it derives from the Latin word *cubitum*, meaning 'elbow'. This measurement was used throughout the ancient world. As its name suggests, it was based upon the length of a forearm, from middle fingertip to the crook of the elbow. Indeed the hieroglyph representing the cubit is a pictogram of a forearm. The cubit was thought to have originated in Egypt in around 3000 BCE. Several Ancient Egyptian cubit measuring sticks have been uncovered, providing evidence that the cubit was the first attested metrology tool in human history. The earliest example of a wooden cubit stick has been dated to the Middle Kingdom (1938–*c.* 1630 BCE) but was only found as fragments. Whole stone and wooden cubit sticks were discovered in elite burials dating from the New Kingdom (1539–1075 BCE) and some Late Kingdom cubit sticks were found to have been left as offerings at temples, suggesting they were considered high-value objects. Analysis by archaeologists suggests that the average length of an Egyptian cubit was 52 cm. This was subdivided into 7 palms, which were themselves divided into 4 fingers. Variation in the length of the cubit, caused by variations in the human body, led to the creation of the standardized royal cubit. This was based on the measurement of the forearm of the reigning pharaoh. A black granite version of the royal cubit was created, from which all other cubit sticks could be copied.

The cubit spread from Egypt and was used across the Middle East. The earliest textual reference to a cubit is in the (now fragmentary) *Epic of Gilgamesh*, which was found written in Akkadian on twelve tablets found at Nineveh in the library of Ashur-banipal, king of Assyria (669–631? BCE). Cubits are also mentioned a number of times in the Bible, including memorably in Genesis 6:13–15, when God instructs Noah to build the ark: 'This is how you are to make it: the length of the ark three hundred cubits, its breadth fifty cubits, and its height thirty cubits.' From the Middle East the cubit's use spread into the Greek and Roman worlds, and through their wide-ranging empires and extensive trade networks the cubit became somewhat standardized. The length continued to vary from region to region but it was still ostensibly based on the distance between a man's middle fingertip and his elbow. Archaeological evidence suggests that Middle East cubits ranged from 44 cm to 52.5 cm. The smaller type is generally known as the short or anthropological cubit and the larger is known as the long or architectural cubit. In the Islamic world the cubit was known as *dhirā* and varied from 48 cm to 145 cm depending on the region. It was subdivided into 2 Arabic feet. The *dhirā* was used right up to the medieval period.

Across the Roman Empire the 'natural' cubit of around 1.5 feet or 45 cm was widely used, reiterating the cubit's continued association with the length of an average man's forearm. The cubit was used in Europe up until the Renaissance, as attested by the autobiography of the sculptor Benvenuto Cellini (1500–1571), who recounted that when casting his figure of Perseus holding the head of Medusa he used the cubit as the measure of length. However, the cubit was never fully standardized and over time it fell from use as most Europeans favoured the foot or the yard. Many scholars, however, continue to be fascinated by the historical cubit and have worked on deciphering its exact length. Unfortunately

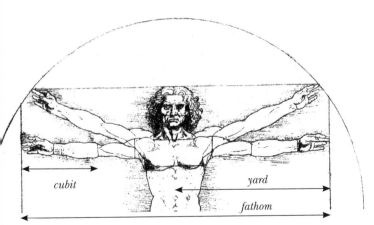

cubit

yard

fathom

geographical variance was rife and, so determining a single standard cubit is not possible, but most scholars agree that the most frequently used value was from 18 to 20 inches. In the age of scientific accuracy the rather vague, anthropocentric cubit has faded from use in favour of the more reliable metric measures. However, the use of a forearm to make rough estimates of length remains one of the most widely available, and indeed portable, measures there is.

Ell

The ell was a measurement used across northern Europe. It was thought to derive from the cubit, as an ell was originally based on the length of a man's forearm and outstretched hand. The term 'ell' likely comes from the Latin *ulna*, meaning forearm; in Old English it was *eln*, meaning length of the arm, which serves as the same root for the word 'elbow'. Although the ell derived from the length of a forearm (roughly 18 inches), over time it came to represent a longer measure and became fairly interchangeable with the yard. By the medieval period, however, the ell became more specifically tied to the measuring of cloth. In the cloth-making regions of northern Europe each area developed its own ell measure, including the Flemish ell of 27 inches, the Scottish ell of 37.1 inches, the English ell of 45 inches and the French ell of 54 inches. In 1196 Richard I issued the Assize of Cloth, which specified that all woollen cloth in England should be made the same size, with a width of 2 ells. Rods of wood known as ellwands were used to delineate the measure, and Edward I of England (r. 1272–1307) decreed that every town in England must have one. Officials known as 'aulnagers' were employed to travel across England measuring cloth at markets. Any cloth found that did not meet the correct measure was forfeit to the Crown. Originally most cloth woven on a hand loom was 27 inches in width – said to be the distance it is comfortable to throw the shuttle from hand to hand. However, some skilled English weavers began to make a broad cloth 45 inches wide, which became especially sought after. It is thought that it was this development which customarily set the English ell at 45 inches. English merchants were used to dealing with different regional ells; those who imported Dutch textiles would use the Flemish ell, while those exporting English linen employed the English ell. In England the ell was never officially standardized and in 1824 when all traditional weights and measures were reviewed by Parliament it was decided that the ell should be rejected as an official English measurement, probably because it was only used in the cloth trade.

In Scotland the ell was initially just over 37 inches (94 cm) and this was standardized in 1661 with an exemplar kept at Edinburgh. Evidence of the importance of the ell in Scotland can be seen in a couple of locations where physical examples of the ell survive, hewn into the fabric of the local market-place; for example, in Dunkeld and Fettercairn. Probably the most famous Scottish ell is preserved at Dornoch Cathedral graveyard. The Plaiden ell, as it is known, is a long flat stone in the ground with two metal points which give the measure of an ell. In the medieval period fairs were regularly held at this location. Like other traditional Scottish marketplaces, it had three important components: a market cross, a weight beam and an ell measure. The market cross was a symbol to all who came to trade at the fair that they would get fair prices. It also sometimes had measures etched onto it: for instance, the Kincardine market cross in the market square at Fettercairn has an ell measure scratched onto its shaft. The weight beam, or tron, offered a place where local authorities could weigh goods brought to the market. Likewise the ell measure was used to check the measure of the cloths which were being traded in the marketplace. The three components of the Scottish marketplace gave traders and buyers alike confidence that they were getting fair prices and made sure that the local authorities could regulate local markets. The ell fell out of use in Scotland in 1824 when English measures (which no longer officially included the ell) were imposed on Scotland.

Yard

The yard was a traditional English unit of length which gets its name from the Old English *gerd*, meaning rod or measuring stick. It was thought to have been originally based on the diameter of an average man's waist or his belt, although some scholars point to a more ancient origin and argue that the yard represents a double cubit. The yard was traditionally broken down into the half-yard, span, finger and nail. The *Chronicles* of William of Malmesbury tell us that King Henry I (r. 1100–1135) decreed that 'false yards' should be counteracted by creating a standard yard based on the distance between his own nose and the thumb of his out-stretched arm. By 1306 the yard was defined more closely in relation to the existing measures of feet and inches, with the 1311 compilation of charters, statues and decrees, the *Liber Horn*, stating: 'And be it remembered that the iron yard of our Lord the King containeth 3 feet and no more, and a foot ought to contain 12 inches by the right measure of this yard measured.' This refers to the iron rods that were used as standard yards. The originals would be kept by the monarch and copies sent to each region as a way to keep measures standard throughout the land.

The Science Museum in London holds one of the standard yards created during the reign of Elizabeth I (1558–1603). It is made of bronze and has a square-shaped cross-section. These bars were kept at the Exchequer and copies were sent out to each borough. Elizabeth's yard was considered accurate enough to be used until 1824, when the Imperial Measures Act required new ones to be issued. These new standards did not last long as they were destroyed during a fire at the Houses of Parliament in 1834. In 1845 forty new standards were constructed from an alloy of copper, tin and zinc, selected for its durability by the astronomer Francis Baily before his death in 1844. The standards were 36 inches long and 1 inch square. To ensure accuracy when manufacturing the bars, their maker, his successor, Rev. Richard Sheepshanks, had a special new super-accurate thermometer constructed; to limit thermal expansion and to prevent bending he floated the bars in vats of mercury as they were being measured. One, considered to be the most accurate, was selected to be the official imperial yard. The others were sent out to various cities and institutions, including the Royal Mint and the Royal Society of London. The new imperial standard was thereafter kept in a fireproof box (and was originally bricked into the walls of the Palace of Westminster); it was remeasured and checked for accuracy every twenty years.

The yard was adopted as an official standard measure in America in 1832. The standard was taken from a long brass bar made by instrument-makers Troughton of London, which had been transported to America in 1815. The yard was officially said to be the distance between the 27th and the 63rd inches on this brass bar. A new standard arrived from Britain in 1856. When it was compared with the Troughton standard, it was found to be marginally shorter. This indicated that the old Troughton standard was now inaccurate and so it was replaced with the new bronze standard from Britain.

Metal rods tend to shrink over time, and so by the nineteenth century it was decided that the yard should be measured in relation to a metre. In 1895 it was agreed that the length of the metre was 39.370113 inches relative to the imperial standard yard. In 1959 this was refined further when an agreement was made between the United States of America, Canada, Australia, New Zealand, South Africa and the United Kingdom that a yard should be officially defined as 0.9144 of a metre.

Today most British people encounter yards only as a colloquial way of giving a rough estimate of distance, because most official measuring apparatus today uses centimetres and metres, often alongside inches and feet. Like many of the older customary measures, the use of yards has become generational, with most people under the age of 60 never having been taught measurement in yards and only understanding it from their parents' and grandparents' use of the term.

The word 'yard' meaning outdoor space adjacent to a building, and seen in related words 'courtyard', 'graveyard', 'barnyard and so on, is not in fact related to the old measurement. Instead this yard derives from the Old English *geard*, which is also the root word for garden.

Mensura Christi

Theologians of both the Eastern and Western Churches became preoccupied during the early medieval period with the true height of Jesus Christ. Although unlikely to have ever been used as an actual measurement, representations of the physical height of Christ were thought to bring a sense of his physical presence and were therefore treated as sacred objects. The story of how these estimates of Christ's height were arrived at lend some insight into early visualizations of length. One early example of a representation of Christ's height came from the Byzantine emperor Justinian (r. 527–565), who sent three trusted men to measure the impression of Christ left on the Turin Shroud. The height they recorded has been given as 183.5 centimetres in modern measurements. It was said that from this measurement a life-size cross was built, made of silver, coated with gold and encrusted with precious gems. This cross, sometimes known as the Measuring Cross, was kept in the sacristy of the Hagia Sophia in Istanbul alongside other relics of the crucifixion such as the nails and a sample of the True Cross. Unfortunately in 1204 during the sacking of Constantinople the 'Measuring Cross' was stolen and its fate remains unknown. However, the references to it in medieval texts remain, such as the twelfth-century *mensura Christi* manuscript kept in the Laurentian Library, Florence (Codice 3 of Pluteus 25). This parchment contains an illustration of Christ with a decorated line underneath it. An inscription states that the length of the line beneath the illustration is one-twelfth of the height of Christ and that this measurement was taken from the Measuring Cross.

In the Western Church a similar physical embodiment of the height of Christ was contrived; this one still stands in the Basilica of St John Lateran in Rome. Here four marble pillars of uncertain date are said to represent the height of Christ's body and measure 183 cm. On top of the pillars rests a granite slab, which also lays claims to some biblical history. The slab is said to be the table top on which the thirty pieces of silver were passed to Judas. The *mensura Christi* in St John Lateran was thought to have been brought to Rome by Emperor Constantine's mother, Helen, which would date it to the early fourth century CE.

Aside from the Turin Shroud, estimates of Christ's height were also given based on the rock on which Christ's body was laid to rest, known as *locus Dominici Corporis*. Christ's tomb was first identified by envoys of Emperor Constantine in *c.*325 CE. Today it forms part of one of the most holy Christian sites at the Holy Sepulchre Church in Jerusalem. In 2016 archaeologists were given just sixty hours to investigate the tomb and in that time lifted a number of marble slabs to see the actual rock-hewn grave beneath. Historically a number of early sources, such as the Venerable Bede in 735 and Haymo, Bishop of Halberstadt (d. 853), gave the dimensions of the Holy Sepulchre from which estimations of Christ's height were given.

By the sixth century lengths of material were being sold in Jerusalem which were said to be based on Christ's height. Similarly, ribbons 183 cm long and based on the Turin Shroud were also created and used as lucky amulets. More recently estimates of Christ's height have been based not on holy relics but instead by looking at skeletons of the typical man of the time from Judea and Egypt. These estimates gave Christ a smaller stature of around 170 cm. The continued efforts to conjure an accurate height for Christ reveals the enduring desire to lend physical heft to the body of Christ, perhaps because it allows worshippers to visualize his reassuring physical presence.

Furlong

The furlong is an measure of distance deriving from the medieval open-field farming system. The term neatly reveals its relationship to the land, coming from the Old English *furlang* – from *furh*, meaning 'furrow', and *lang*, 'long'. During the Middle Ages in England the open-field system was the predominant method of land management. Each village or manor had a number of large open fields to farm. These 'great fields' were divided into narrow strips, known as selions, which were farmed by tenants. The strips of land were measured in furlongs, traditionally the distance a team of two oxen could plough without resting. This cooperative method of farming divided up huge swathes of arable land between local tenants, and resulted in distinctive ridge and furrow patterns. These patterns were created by ploughs; the method ensured that each strip of land was clearly defined and provided with good drainage. When viewed from above, medieval ridge-and-furrow fields often appear in an *S* or a *C* shape, which was created by the turning of the oxen at the end of each furrow. The furlongs in these fields could be as long as 700 metres, depending on the quality of the soil and the method of ploughing, and the ridges ranged in width from 5 to 20 metres. Because furlongs were a

key method of measuring land (they were used as a measure in the Domesday Book in 1086) and vital to English land deeds, it became important that they were standardized. It was decreed that a furlong was 40 rods or 10 chains. Even as other measurements changed around them, the furlong stayed essentially the same, with only its relationship to other measures adapting.

Initially the Saxons used the North German foot, longer than the modern foot, but between 1266 and 1303 the Statute of Ells and Perches saw a number of English measures codified, including the foot, which was set as 12 inches. The definition of a rod therefore changed from 15 old feet to 16.5 new feet. This in turn meant that the furlong now contained 660 new feet, rather than 600 old feet. The mile was also redefined at this time. It was deemed important to keep its relationship to old Roman measures. The furlong was considered to be equivalent to a Roman *stade*, of which there were 8 in a mile. This meant that when the mile was redefined in England it was kept as it always had been, at 8 furlongs. However, the definition of the mile itself changed to 5,280 feet, or 8 furlongs made up of 40 rods at 16.5 feet a rod. For many years the furlong remained a key measure of distance for land measurement, but it was little used in other contexts, where feet, yards and miles were preferred.

The furlong was officially abolished as an accepted measurement in England in 1985 but persists in the context of horse racing. This is because when horse racing was formalized in the sixteenth century and the first racing tracks were established the furlong was still a common form of land measurement. Notably only horse races of less than a mile are referred to in furlongs – so a race of three-quarters of a mile would be known as a 6-furlong race, but a race of a mile and a half would be called just that, rather than 12 furlongs or 1 mile and 4 furlongs.

Rod, pole, perch & chain

The rod, pole and perch were terms used to describe one of the basic physical land measures used by surveyors since the medieval period. The terms were all used interchangeably across England, each having its own root. 'Rod' comes from the Old English *rodd*, which itself comes from the Old Norse *rudda*, which meant 'club'. 'Pole' comes from Old English *pal*, which itself had a Germanic root, deriving from the Old Saxon *pal*, meaning 'stake'. 'Perch' comes from the French *perche*, which comes from the Latin *pertica*, meaning 'long pole' or 'measuring rod'. In the Middle Ages it became increasingly important for tenant farmers to be able to accurately delineate the land they were renting. As a result surveyors responsible for recording area in land deeds would use actual long wooden poles which they would lay out on the ground to measure. Although the size varied regionally, the rod became roughly standardized to around 5.5 yards or 16 feet 6 inches, as this was the largest size which could be handled safely while remaining relatively straight.

Some sources suggest that the pole was equivalent in length to a military lance, and others suggest that they were a similar size to the sticks used to drive the oxen pulling a plough, but no definitive evidence exists to suggest the measuring rod was based on either of these items. Rods were clearly a recognized form of measure in the thirteenth century, when they were used to standardize the acre (4 rods by 40 rods), and were commonly used up until the eighteenth century. One creative method for ascertaining the correct length of a rod was suggested in 1536 by German mathematician Jacob Köbel:

> Take sixteen men, short men and tall ones as they leave church and let each of them put one shoe after the other and the length thus obtained shall be a just and common measuring rod to survey the land with.

More commonly, though, the rod was standardized as a length of 16.5 feet and continued to be an actual physical wooden rod, used by surveyors in the field. However, as scientific innovations required greater accuracy from the 1700s the fallibility of using wooden rods in the damp English climate became apparent. Surveyor William Roy was tasked in 1784 with measuring a base line from Hampton Poor House to Hounslow Heath to enable a triangulation to determine the precise size of a degree of latitude. This measure ultimately became the triangulation upon which all Ordnance Survey maps were subsequently based. Roy initially used a wooden rod made from New England pine and cut from a ship's mast, but this was deemed too inaccurate in the damp English weather and so he switched to using three glass tubes, each 20 feet long, balanced on wooden cradles. This was surprisingly accurate. When the 5 miles were remeasured eight years later the measurement was found to be only 2¾ inches (7 cm) out.

In 1620 English clergyman and mathematician Edmund Gunter (1581–1626) introduced Gunter's Chain. Gunter pioneered land surveying by measuring the length between two topographical features and then using triangulation to calculate the area. To make measuring easier, Gunter invented a linked steel chain which when laid out flat was 66 feet long (equivalent to 4 rods or 20 metres) and was made from 100 links. The chain was marked every ten links using brass tags to enable intermediate measurements to be taken. The beauty of the chain was that it could be folded up easily and transported as the surveyor travelled from job to job. Crucially the chain also married up with the acre, because 1 acre was 10 chains by 10 chains. Metal chains soon superseded the wooden rod as the favoured method of land measurement. Between 1633 and 1635 surveyor Richard Norwood demonstrated the chain's accuracy by measuring the distance between London and York (accounting for twists and turns, ascents and descents) and came up with a distance of 179 miles (only 600 yards too long). The chain and link (each link being one-hundredth of a chain) became standard land surveying measures in Britain; as the Empire expanded these measurements were adopted in the colonies. In 1785 the Public Land Survey Ordinance was adopted in America, which mandated links, chains and miles as the basic units of measurement for land surveys. This meant that all US townships built during this period were laid out in chains. Over time, as developments such as the metal measuring tape were introduced and greater accuracy in land measurement was achieved, the chain as a unit of measure fell out of fashion in favour of metric measures. However, chains still appear as an echo in various parts of British life. On cricket pitches, for example, the distance between the wickets is 1 chain (20 metres). Likewise when the railways were built across Britain the chain was used as measurement. This persists through 'chainage', a method to signpost topographical features on the railway lines. For example, a tunnel or bridge will be marked with a sign showing how many miles and chains it is from the start of the line. This allows engineers to identify which exact feature they need to inspect.

Today surveyors use super-accurate lasers to measure the distance between two points. These are recorded in clearly defined metres. The old customary measures based on the physical measuring instruments of earlier surveyors have therefore gone the way of the equipment itself and become obsolete.

Acre, oxgang, virgate, carucate & hide

In the medieval period agricultural land measurement was generally based on practical considerations. The word 'acre' comes from the Old English *æcer*, which in Middle English became *aker*, and is akin to the Latin *ager*, all of which mean 'field'. An acre was defined as the length of 1 furlong (660 feet) and the width of 4 rods (66 feet), as this was the area of land it was thought that a single ploughman could work in one day. This would work out as a farmer and their oxen ploughing the length of a furlong 66 times in one day (66 × 660 feet), which gives the area of an acre as 43,560 square feet. However, when basing the acre on its traditional definition of how much a farmer can plough in one day, any number of variables are introduced which can affect how large that acre is. Is the farmer young and healthy or old and infirm? Are the oxen biddable or lazy? Is the land flat and even, or hilly and full of stones? All of these factors mean that the size of a traditional acre could vary greatly.

The acre became standardized in the reign of Edward I (r. 1272–1307) when it was defined in relation to other measures. From this point onwards an acre was described as 4 rods by 40 rods (4,840 square yards or 43,560 square feet), thereby becoming a definite area of land rather than a notional one. Historically the acre has long been the main method of recording land measurement in England, with deeds describing the area of land held by a landowner or householder in acres. Traditionally the acre is based on an area of land, not its shape, meaning that an acre can be any shape as long as it is 4,840 square yards.

Other traditional English land measurements were also based on the plough. An 'oxgang' was described as the amount of land that could be tilled by one ox in the course of a ploughing season. It was equivalent to the Norman *bovate*. In some contexts the area of an oxgang or oxgate was also supposed to include enough land on which to grow food to support the ox. These areas of land might consist of a number of different parcels of land which together were deemed to create an oxgang. The term was used to calculate a tenant's responsibility and work out how much tax or rates they should pay. It was well accepted that the area which an oxgang represented can and did vary significantly. A document from Leeds in 1628 states: 'what Acres an oxegange doth Conteyne we Cannot Certainlie sett downe', but an oxgang usually covered from 15 to 20 acres.

A 'virgate' was another traditional English plough-related measure of land, generally used for taxation purposes. It was held to be the amount of land that two oxen could plough in a season and was equivalent to a quarter of a hide, which meant it was commonly accepted to be around 30 acres. The term comes from the Old English *gyrd lands*, which means a yard of land, but isn't linked to the yard measure but rather the stick used to measure acres, known as the rod.

In the areas of England covered by Danelaw (the area which today includes the following modern shires: Leicester, York, Nottingham, Derby, Lincoln, Essex, Cambridge, Suffolk, Norfolk, Northampton, Huntingdon, Bedford, Hertford, Middlesex and Buckingham) and therefore under the control of the Danes and their customary laws, an area of land which could be ploughed by a team of eight oxen in a ploughing season was known as a 'carucate'. The term comes from *carruca*, which was a type of heavy plough introduced in the ninth century. A carucate was usually 120 acres and the tax levied on each carucate was known as 'carucage'. For the rest of England 120 acres were generally known as a 'hide'. The definition of a hide was not based on the plough but instead on the area of land deemed sufficient to support one family or household for a year. Hides were used to calculate land tax and other public obligations, such as maintenance of fortifications, and were used up until the twelfth century. They weren't really linked to an area of land but rather to the value of that land, and so one hide for taxable purposes might be subdivided among a number of people who farmed smaller parcels of land within it. Up until the twelfth century the hide was used across England to levy taxes, but because its relationship to an actual area of land varied so widely historians now demur from tying it to a specific measurement.

Fathom

A 'fathom' is an Old English measurement which today is usually used to describe the depth of water. Traditionally a fathom is the distance between the very tips of a man's outstretched arms and this is reflected in the word's etymology. The word has a Germanic origin and comes via the Old Saxon *fathmos*, meaning 'outstretched arms'. This developed into the Old English *fæðm*, which meant both 'arms', 'grasp', 'embrace' and 'length of the outstretched arms'. A similar measure was used in Ancient Greece and known as *orguia*. Like many ancient measures related to human body parts, the fathom was not standard but varied from person to person depending on the width of their body span. Over time, however, it came to be customarily accepted that a fathom was equivalent to 6 feet (180 cm). By the sixteenth century the phrase 'fathoming out' is found in printed sources, meaning to measure the size of something using your outstretched arms. This is likely the root of the word being used in an expressive sense to mean trying to figure something out, as in 'I can't fathom what the fellow is getting at.' This also provides a link to sounding things out, which was a method used for measuring depth, usually of water. Sounding out and fathoming out were both used interchangeably by the seventeenth century to mean measuring the depth of water from the side of a ship by using a weighted 'sounding' line marked with fathoms. Water, usually of a depth of more than 100 fathoms and therefore too deep to measure with a sounding line, was usually described by sailors as 'off soundings'. In this way fathoms came to be considered a nautical measure, and as such the British Admiralty officially defined the fathom as a thousandth of an imperial nautical mile, which made it 6.08 feet (1.85 m). However, the customary 6 foot fathom was still the preferred measure for most British and American seamen.

Fathoms are also used in a number of different contexts. For line fishermen fathoms were used to measure line length, with the very long lines often divided into 50 fathom 'lines'. The depths of mine-shafts in the UK were also measured in fathoms up until the early twentieth century. The fathom has largely gone out of fashion as a measurement and it was never given an international standard. But it lingers on as an expression; for example, 'I can't fathom why the fathom went out of fashion.'

Mile

Today the mile, at 5,280 feet or 1,760 yards, seems like a relatively arbitrary measurement and yet it is still widely used across Britain and America. Most Brits and Americans can easily visualize a mile and it is most often used to give an impression of distance – when asked how far the nearest shop is, most would respond in miles rather than the more universally recognized kilometres. Indeed, despite widespread metrification, road signs and speed limits in Britain and America are still displayed in miles and miles per hour.

The origin of the mile can be traced back to the Romans. Most ancient measurements were based upon the human body, and the mile is no different. The Roman mile (*mille passus*) was described as a thousand paces. Paces were measured as every other time the foot hit the ground, or, to put it more simply, each time the left foot hit the ground was counted as one pace. In 29 BCE the Roman mile was further standardized when Roman general Agrippa (63–12 BCE) decreed that the Roman foot should be modelled on his own foot, with a length of 0.971 feet (29.6 cm). This would give Agrippa a hefty size 12 shoe in UK sizes (or 12.5 in US sizes and 46 in EU sizes). The Roman mile was then measured as 5,000

Roman feet, meaning that each pace was 5 Roman feet (148 cm). The mile was an important measurement for the Romans and it spread widely throughout their empire. A mile marker was placed in the Forum in Rome by Emperor Caesar Augustus which became known as *Milliarium Aureum*, the 'Golden Milestone', and it was from here that every Roman road in the network was considered to start, thereby giving us the phrase 'all roads lead to Rome'. The Golden Milestone was thought to have been crafted in marble or bronze but its exact location has been lost, although some historians suggest that a marble structure in the Roman Forum could well be the base of the missing monument. Across the Empire milestones were placed at the side of roads every 1,000 paces and marked either with the name of the current emperor or with a Roman numeral indicating how many miles it was to the nearest town or village. A large number of these milestones have survived, providing a reminder of the scope of the Roman Empire. The word 'milestone' has also been adopted colloquially to represent the step along a long road. For example,

one might say that buying your first pint of beer in a pub constitutes an important milestone for any young Briton.

In Greece and the Byzantine Empire the Roman mile came to be used in tandem with the native Greek mile, or 600 Greek feet (*pous*). It was, however, fairly unstandardized as the measurement varied from region to region, meaning that the Athenian foot at 31.6 cm was larger than the Minoan foot at 30.4 cm. The Greek mile was known as *milion* and was 5,000 Greek feet long (which, as discussed above, was something of a movable feast). Like the Golden Milestone in Rome, Constantine had a monument raised in Constantinople in the fourth century CE to be the starting point from which all roads in the Byzantine Empire began. By the sixteenth century the monument had been destroyed, but traces of it were uncovered in the 1960s near the Hagia Sophia.

As a former part of the Roman Empire, Britain had adopted the Roman mile but by the medieval period its length had become more associated with the Anglo-Saxon furlong (see page 75). An English mile was considered to be 8 furlongs long (5,280 feet), which was a bit awkward as it did not match up with the Continental Roman mile. As a result in 1593 it was decided that the English statute mile should be standardized at 8 furlongs/320 poles/1,760 yards. This ought to have settled things, but unfortunately map-makers continued to use local measurements, and evidence from some of the earliest maps of Britain held in the Bodleian Library in Oxford reveal that the English mile varied from 7 to 10 furlongs in length. Wales, Scotland and Ireland all also had their own local definitions of a mile, which were used in tandem with the statute mile up until 1824 when the Weights and Measures Act made the statute mile standard across the United Kingdom and Ireland.

In 1959, after it was realized that the mile differed slightly in length between the largest countries still using the measurement, it was decided that an 'international mile' should be agreed. The United States, the United Kingdom, Canada, Australia, New Zealand and South Africa signed up to the international yard and pound agreement which specified that a yard was 0.9144 metres in length, making an international mile 1,609.344 metres.

The nautical mile was developed by navigators at sea in the sixteenth century and is measured in relation to the Earth's equator. If you picture the Earth as an orange which is sliced in half, the equator is the circle produced by the cut edge. This can be divided into 360 degrees. One degree of that circle is 60 minutes and 1 minute of that arc (also known as an arc minute) is a nautical mile. However, as the Earth has slightly flattened poles a minute of latitude is not constant. As a result the nautical mile was slightly different across nations, with France using the definition of a metre as standardized in 1791 at one ten-millionth of a quarter meridian, which placed their nautical mile at 1,852 metres; whereas America and Britain used an average arc minute, meaning their nautical mile was 1,853 metres. To clear this up, in 1929 the international nautical mile was introduced, which was defined as 1,852 metres. However, it took until 1954 for the Americans and 1970 for the British to officially accept this.

Colloquially, since at least the 1800s, people in the English-speaking world have used the phrase 'a country mile' to mean a very long way. For example, you might say Usain Bolt beat the rest of the field by a country mile. The exact etymology of this term is disputed but one of the more credible explanations given is that although a distance might be 1 mile as the crow flies, were you to walk the distance down winding country roads you would actually travel considerably further.

Despite metrification being officially embraced by the British government in 1965 many imperial measures have persisted, and the mile is one such example. Similarly America has never officially adopted the metric system. It seems likely that with no pressing need to change, the mile will continue to be the main way to measure the distance by road and the speed of vehicles in both Britain and America.

Centimetre, metre
& kilometre

The centimetre, metre and kilometre all originate in the development of the metric system. In 1670 Gabriel Mouton, a priest and passionate mathematician from Lyon in France, proposed the creation of a decimal system of measurement. In Mouton's system, measurements would be based on the swing of a pendulum. He believed that nature provided perfect regularity and that this should be used to create a new, logical system of measurement. Mouton suggested various length measurements, including *mille*, based on the length of the arc of one second of longitude at the equator on the Earth's surface and divided decimally. Mouton's ideas were taken seriously by scholars, with both Jean Picard and Christiaan Huygens coming out in favour of his suggestion. Similarly the Royal Society in London discussed and debated his proposal. However, it would be more than a hundred years before any such decimal system would be fully developed and adopted.

The French Revolution provided the impetus to do away with the existing confusing array of regional measurements and royal standards. This was an opportunity to come up with a rational system of measurements based on multiples of ten. In 1791 the French National Assembly asked the French Academy of Sciences to develop a working system. After much debate they decided to base the decimal system on the length of one ten-millionth of a quadrant of a great circle of Earth, measured around the poles of the meridian passing through Paris, or, to put it more simply, a fraction of the distance from the North Pole to the equator.

To ascertain the value of the measure, the arc of the meridian between Barcelona in Spain and Dunkirk in France needed to be measured. This was to be known as the Paris meridian, and the Paris Observatory has a brass strip laid into the marble floor of the Meridian Room which shows where the line of longitude runs through France's capital city. It took a team of astronomers seven long years to survey the area and then through triangulation to work out the meridian arc.

From these measurements the team finally came up with a measure for the new base unit. They proposed to call it the metre, from the Greek word *metron*, meaning 'measure', and declared that it was 39.37008 inches long. A platinum version of this metre length was created and stored at the French National Archives as the first standard metre. Each metre was to be made up of 100 centimetres and each centimetre was made up of 10 millimetres. Any country adopting the metre was also taking on its constituent parts. In 1801 the metric system became the only system of measure allowed in France, but this was not to last long. Napoleon revoked the law in 1812 and returned to customary measures, albeit adapted to become multiples of the metric system. Some years after Napoleon's defeat, the metric system was once again introduced into France in 1840.

Other countries soon followed suit and began adopting the metric system and making copies of the platinum metre in the French National Archives, known as the *mètre des Archives*. However, it soon became clear that the copies were not always accurate and that the standard *mètre des Archives* itself might be degrading over time, leaving the exact length of the metre in doubt. In 1867 it was proposed that a new international standard metre should be created, but it took many years and much discussion before it came to fruition. An international treaty known as the Convention du Mètre was signed by seventeen states in 1875, agreeing to a standard metre and resulting in a new standard of 90 per cent platinum and 10 per cent iridium being crafted. British firm Johnson Matthey manufactured thirty versions of the metre standard and in 1889 bar number 6 was accepted as the international standard. It was stored by the International Bureau of Weights and Measures (BIPM) while the remainder were sent out to be standards in other signatory states. Work continued to try to come up with a more easily duplicated measure of the metre, and in 1960 it was agreed that a metre should be defined as 1,650,763.73 wavelengths of orange-red light, produced by burning the element krypton (isotope Kr-86), in a vacuum. By 1983, following the invention of lasers and developments in electronics, it became possible to define a metre in relation to the speed of light. The metre, it was decreed, should be defined as the path travelled by light in a vacuum in one 299,792,458th of a second. It was now possible using lasers and sensitive measurement devices to recreate an exact metre standard in any laboratory in the world, finally making the dream of creating a standard measure based on immutable natural laws a reality. It is interesting to note that although the US Congress legalized the use of the metric system in 1866, the USA does not use the metre as a measure of length; instead it is used to define the length of the favoured measures of yards, feet and inches.

The kilometre (1,000 metres) also derived from the metre and was adopted in France as a longer measure of length at the same time as the metre was introduced. Initially it was not known as the kilometre but had various different names according to region. In France it was at first known as *millaire*; in the Netherlands it was known as the *mijl*. Over time the kilometre became the accepted standard term and today nearly all countries (except the USA and UK, which use the mile) use kilometres as the standard method of measuring distances over land.

Astronomical units, light years & parsecs

Ever since astronomers first looked up into the sky and marvelled at the celestial bodies, there has been a desire to measure and understand the huge distances involved. Ancient Greek astronomers, such as Aristarchus of Samos and Archimedes in the third century BCE, attempted to estimate the distance between the Earth and the Sun. In China in the first century BCE the mathematical text *Zhoubi Suanjing* suggested the distance between the Sun and the Earth could be calculated using the shadows cast at midday. However, these calculations were based on the supposition that the Earth was flat. By the second century CE, astronomer and mathematician Ptolemy was using trigonometry to work out the radius of the Earth, Moon and Sun. He estimated that the distance between the Earth and the Sun was 1,210 times the radius of the Earth, an assertion that was taken as canonical by medieval European and Islamic astronomers.

By the seventeenth century, after the invention of the telescope and the discovery of Kepler's Laws of Planetary Motion, it became possible to revisit planetary distances. Astronomers were now able to create a proportional model of objects in orbit around the Sun. These models did not relate to a particular scale but instead made sense of the objects in relation to one another.

It was around this time that the need for an 'astronomical unit' (AU), which could be used to understand the vast distances between objects in the solar system, was accepted. It was agreed that the parallax method would be the most accurate way of working out the distance between the Earth and the Sun, which could then be applied as 1 astronomical unit. Parallax is the seeming displacement of an object due to a change in the observer's point of view. It can be neatly explained by holding your finger out in front of you and closing your left eye, then switching and opening your left eye while closing your right. Your finger will appear to shift slightly against the background. By measuring this small shift in position and knowing the distance between your eyes, you can use trigonometry to work out the distance between you and your outstretched finger.

This effect can be applied to measuring distances between planets and astronomical objects. The orbit of the Earth around the Sun is used as the baseline, and so observations of the astronomical object in question are taken in relation to the distant stars in the background. Six months later these same observations are repeated and recorded. The apparent change in the object's position can then be used to work out its distance from the Earth.

In 1838 Friedrich Bessel calculated the distance between Earth and the star 61 Cygni using parallax, becoming the first person to use the method to calculate the distance to a star. Bessel expressed the value in AU, and added that it would take light 10.3 years to travel the distance. In this way he introduced the concept of light years and provided a new way to think about these vast distances. Light at this time was not considered a constant of nature, and the speed of light was not accurately known, but it would become clearer in the coming decades. Otto Ule used the term *Lichtjahr*, 'light year', as an astronomical measure of distance for the first time in an article in 1851. This set the meaning of the term as the distance you could travel in a year if you could travel at the speed of light. In 1905 Einstein's Theory of Special Relativity indicated that light always travels at the same speed. The speed of light was now accepted as a constant and so became a useful method for measuring great distances. Today a light year is considered the distance that a photon of light can travel in one year, which is about 9 trillion kilometres, 6 trillion miles or 63,000 AU.

The development of the light year to discuss huge interplanetary distances also encouraged the creation of an official astronomical unit representing the distance between the Earth and the Sun; the term AU was first used in 1903. As technological innovations stacked up, measurements became increasingly accurate. By the 1960s, when radar telemetry had been developed and space exploration had commenced, precise measurements of the distance between the Earth and planets and objects in the solar system were achieved. The International Astronomical Union (IAU) officially adopted a new definition of an astronomical unit in 1976, and over the coming years it continued to be updated as improved technology brought ever more accurate measurements. The calculations for an AU are extremely complex. Put simply, today 1 AU is considered to be around 93 million miles (150 million kilometres). Astronomical units allow huge distances to be expressed simply and can help to view the distances involved in relative terms. For example, the distance from the Earth to the Sun is 1 AU, whereas the distance from the Sun to Saturn's orbit is 9.5 AU (or a mind-boggling 886,000,000 miles).

The final part of the astronomical measurements puzzle is the 'parsec'. This vast unit is used to measure the distance to astronomical objects outside our solar system. A parsec is essentially equal to 3.26 light years, or 206,000 astronomical units. The word 'parsec' was coined by astronomer Herbert Hall Turner in 1913; it is formed as a portmanteau of 'parallax of

one second', parsecs being calculated using trigonometry and parallax. Due to the complexity of
understanding and working out distances in parsecs
the term is generally only used by astrophysicists and
astronomers.

VOLUME

'No person will deny that the highest degree of attainable accuracy is an object to be desired, and it is generally found that the last advances towards precision require a greater devotion of time, labour, and expense, than those which precede them.'

CHARLES BABBAGE

Fluid apothecary units

The English apothecaries' system for measuring volume developed from the Roman system and was used by apothecaries and physicians for dispensing medicine. The amounts of fluid volume were usually small in comparison with trade volumes, which were more usually transported and sold in multiple gallons. Apothecary weights are similar to the troy system of weights, with the grain and the pound in both systems having equivalent values. Recipes for medicines were generally written out in Latin and had their own system of shorthand to denote the weights and measures required.

The apothecaries' fluid volume was equivalent to apothecary weights, so it was based on the ounce, which in the fluid system is known as a fluid ounce. A fluid ounce is the volume of an ounce of water. Fluid ounces are divided into fluid drachms, the weight of a drachm, and are further divided into fluid scruples and minims, the equivalent of the grain. The fluid system initially included a measure known as 'the drop', which was the amount of liquid that would fall from a bottle in one drop. However, as you might imagine, this differed wildly in volume from bottle to bottle, liquid to liquid, and so for accuracy's sake the minim was preferred as the smallest unit. The minim was still seen, however, as equivalent to one drop of water. A fluid dram is made up of 60 minims, and 1 fluid ounce of 8 fluid drams (or 480 minims). The apothecaries' system officially coexisted as a system of measuring volume in England until it was decreed in 1858 that the avoirdupois system of weights and measures should be used in its stead. Many pharmacists continued to work with the familiar apothecaries' system to dispense medicines until 1 January 1971, when the metric system was officially adopted across all sectors in Britain.

Traditional medicinal recipe books known as pharmacopoeias were used until around 1900. In these volumes recipes were given in Latin using the apothecaries' system. Alongside the 'official' terms they also sometimes employed other rough measures of volume, including the teaspoon (see page 135), the wine glass and the teacup. It was only as medical science advanced and drugs began to be mass-produced rather than mixed by the local apothecary that more accurate measurements were required. Today in the UK drugs are dispensed in millilitres and micrograms to ensure absolute accuracy.

Pint

The pint was a common measure of liquid volume across Europe from the fourteenth century. The word 'pint' reflects its European origins, deriving from the Old French *pinte*, which itself comes from the Vulgar Latin *pincta*, a corruption of the Latin *picta*, meaning 'painted'. It is thought the measure would be 'painted' onto vessels to indicate the size of a pint. The pint is defined as ⅛ of a gallon, but because there have been numerous regional variations on the exact measurement of a gallon this has meant that the size of a pint has also fluctuated across regions and from country to country. A pint can be further divided into 4 gills, a gill being 5 fluid ounces. The size of a modern standard UK pint was set in 1824 when Parliament adopted imperial measurements, defining a gallon as 160 fluid ounces, which made a pint ⅛ of that: 20 fluid ounces. The United States of America, however, had already moved towards British measurements, basing the US customary system on the old English wine measure. This made their liquid gallon 231 cubic inches and set their pint as 16 fluid ounces, which, like the English pint, is equivalent to ⅛ of a gallon – although each system uses its own gallon with differing measures. This is why if a Briton goes into an American bar and orders a pint of beer they might feel rather short-changed as they will be getting a pint of 473 ml, whereas in Britain a pint of beer is 568 ml. The American system also adds another layer of confusion because they also have a 'dry pint', which is used to measure dry goods, such as blueberries, and is *c.* 550 ml. Scotland had its own pint up until the union with England in 1707, which was used for wet and dry goods and was known as the Stirling pint. The Stirling pint towered over the English pint, coming in at the equivalent of 3¼ imperial pints.

Metrification supposedly saw the end of the imperial pint, but it has lingered on our doorsteps in the glass pint milk bottles that continue to be delivered up and down the country – and, of course, in the pub, where the pint is the mainstay of beer and cider drinkers. The pint had been slated to become outlawed in 2009 to make Britain more in line with the rest of the EU, but beer lovers everywhere protested vehemently at the potential loss of the iconic pint of beer. After years of bitter negotiations the European Union graciously conceded the point and allowed Britain to continue using imperial measures alongside metric equivalents.

Since 1824 all official pint glasses in pubs up and down the country have been required to be sandblasted with the crown stamp to prove that they are full pint or half-pint measures. Traditionally pints of beer in England had been consumed in a tankard made from pewter, wood or ceramic. Glass tankards came into popularity in England in around 1928 and by 1938 they had mostly been replaced by the dimpled tankard which many still think of as the classic pint glass. As beer drinking became more commercialized the problem of safely stacking and transporting beer glasses inspired American inventor Hugo Pick in 1913 to develop the conical-shaped beer glass with a bulge near the lip to make it easier to grasp. This design became known as the nonik glass and after its introduction to Britain in 1948 it soon became the most popular style of pint glass in British pubs. The British love affair with the humble pint of beer shows no sign of abating. In fact the variety of drinks that now fill those pints seems to be ever increasing, including bitters, lagers, ales, stouts, ciders and perrys. This indicates that, although we might measure most of our liquids in metric units, when it comes to the pub a pint is still best.

Litre

The French Revolution produced an opportunity for the new government to rationalize the existing chaotic customary system of measurements. In the new Republic, abandoning the old royal standards became possible, something which scientists had been advocating since the seventeenth century. The metric system was science-based, using absolute measurements taken from fundamental natural laws to create a decimal-based order which would allow all measures to be expressed neatly in multiples of ten. The litre (liter in American spelling) was created in 1795 as a measure of volume for liquids. The term came from an existing French unit known as *litron*, which was used as a measure for grain. The litre was based on a cubic decimetre, which is a cube with sides 10 × 10 × 10 cm, whose volume is equivalent to a litre. A litre can be divided into 1,000 millilitres. At the same time the gram was defined as 1 cubic centimetre of water at the temperature of melting ice. As a result 1 litre of liquid water has a mass of nearly 1 kilogram. In 1901 the definition of the litre was changed slightly by the General Conference on Weights and Measures: it became the volume of 1 kilogram of pure water at 4°c at standard atmospheric pressure. This made it fractionally larger than the original definition. However, this move meant that the litre was no longer equivalent to a cubic decimetre and therefore it lost its relationship to the metre. At the 12th General Conference on Weights and Measures in 1964 it was agreed that the original definition of the litre should be reintroduced, ensuring that the volume measure once again was relative to the metre.

At first a lower-case *l* was used as the symbol for a litre. However, this introduced confusion as many people also write the number one (1) as a vertical line and in certain printed fonts lower-case *l* and the number 1 can look almost interchangeable. The International System of Units (SI) has a convention for abbreviations which states that unless the unit is named after an individual then it should be written in lower case. Despite this convention, in 1979 the General Conference on Weights and Measures decreed that for clarity the abbreviation for litres should be a capital *L*. Somewhat curiously, in the United States, and sometimes Canada and Australia, it has become customary to keep the capital *L* when writing out units, so millilitres are expressed as 'mL', whereas across Europe and the rest of the world they are usually given in lowercase as 'ml'. Perhaps because the capital *L* seems incongruous, in Europe drinks packaging often gives the volume fully written out as '1 litre' rather than using the abbreviation.

In 1978 Kenneth Woolner of the University of Waterloo in Ontario, Canada, created an amusing addendum to the history of the litre when he invented the character Claude Émile Jean-Baptiste Litre to account for the capitalization of the measurement's abbreviation. Woolner's colleague Reg Friesen encouraged him to come up with a colourful biography of the fictional character for the April 1978 edition of *Chem 13 News*. Woolner was only too happy to oblige and spent an evening fabricating a fascinating life story for Claude Émile Jean-Baptiste Litre which encompassed encounters with Pierre-Louis Maupertuis and Anders Celsius. The article included amusing captions for the featured illustrations, which Woolner hoped would indicate to his readers that the biography was not quite as it seemed. Most readers got the joke and many wrote in to provide further 'evidence' of Litre's life, adding extra details such as a daughter named Millie. Unfortunately the article was reprinted in a number of other newsletters and journals but without the illustrations, or as an edited, shorter version, and soon Woolner was inundated with letters from librarians requesting sources to back up his biography of Litre. The most widely read reprint of the article appeared in *Chemistry International* in 1980. It was only when the editor was later informed of the mistake and had printed an apology for not noticing the hoax that the amusing affair came to wider attention. Today Claude Émile Jean-Baptiste Litre has his own page on Wikipedia, which makes it clear he is an invented character. Meanwhile *Chem 13 News* regularly reprints the original article, ensuring the delightful hoax lives on.

Gallons, pottles & quarts

The word 'gallon' comes from Old Northern French *galon*, which was also a measure of volume. This in turn was likely related to the Old French word *jale*, which means 'bowl', and the Vulgar Latin *galleta*, which means 'pail' or 'bucket'. The gallon was the basic unit of measurement in England and Wales for a volume of wet or dry goods. Volume is a difficult concept and so originally most measures of volume were based on the dry weight of goods. For example, from 1303 the early gallon in England was defined as the weight of 8 pounds of wheat. Over time the exact volume of a gallon differed, depending on what you were measuring and where. This meant that in Britain there was one gallon for measuring corn, one for ale and one for wine. The corn gallon was also known as the 'Winchester gallon'; it was first officially defined in 1696 as 268.8 cubic inches. The ale gallon was the largest at 282 cubic inches; the wine gallon – also known as 'Queen Anne's gallon', as it was made standard during her reign in 1707 – was the smallest at 231 cubic inches, and was also used to measure oil and honey. America adopted the wine gallon as its standard liquid measure in the early nineteenth century and still uses it. The US gallon is made up of 4 quarts (hence the term, which comes from 'quarter gallon'); each quart (which is equivalent to 1.101220942715 litres) comprises 2 pints. A US pint is 16 US fluid ounces, meaning that 1 fluid ounce is equivalent to $\frac{1}{128}$ of a US gallon.

The Imperial Weights and Measures Act of 1824 got rid of all the various competing gallons in Britain and specified just one, the imperial gallon, which was roughly equivalent to the traditional ale gallon at 277.42 cubic inches. The scientific basis of the French metric system inspired the British to set out a standard for the new imperial gallon, which was decreed as the volume of 10 avoirdupois pounds of distilled water weighed with brass weights in air, with the barometer standing at 30 inches of mercury and a temperature of 62°F. As measurements have been further improved the exact scientific definition of the gallon has been refined a number of times. Like the US gallon, the imperial gallon is made up of 2 pottles (the pottle being equivalent to half a gallon) or 4 quarts, and each quart is composed of 2 pints.

However, as the US and British measurements differ, this makes the imperial quart the equivalent of 1.1365225 litres, which is fractionally different from the US quart. But essentially both US and UK quarts are roughly equivalent to a modern litre.

In 1995 the gallon and the quart became obsolete as official measures in Britain when they were officially replaced by the litre as the primary measure of volume in trade. However, the gallon is still used in a number of British Overseas Territories and Commonwealth countries as the main way of measuring petrol.

Although the gallon may now be seldom used as a measurement in Europe, it lives on in idiom as a way to express a huge amount of liquid. For example, I frequently remark that I drink gallons of tea. Incidentally, the famous 10-gallon cowboy hat does not in fact hold a volume of 10 gallons, but rather is named after the plaited cord which surrounds the hat and comes from the Spanish *galón*, meaning 'braid'.

Wine measures

When Magna Carta was sealed in 1215 it included the plea that wine measures should be standardized. Wine, ale and corn were the only commodities specified in the famous charter, indicating their great importance at that time. Wine has traditionally been kept and traded in barrels of various sizes, each with its own name and relationship to the others. Wine casks have been used since Roman times; traditionally made from white oak, they are constructed from staves of wood held together by wooden or iron hoops. Barrels are shaped with a bulge in the middle, meaning they can be easily rolled along on their side by just one person, even when they are full of liquid. As with most other measurements, barrels were not standardized for a long time and so a variety of different measures sprang up for each size regionally.

The largest wine barrel was known as a tun. It is thought that this is where we get the word 'ton' from for the heaviest weight measure (see page 40). The tun was considered a measure of liquid volume, not weight, and it was used not just for wine but also for oil and honey. The importance of transporting wine, most commonly from France to England, is reflected by the fact that by the 1300s ships were categorized by how many tuns of wine they could hold. A tun

usually consisted of 252 wine gallons, but this varied, with some holding as much as 256 or as little as 208 wine gallons. The next size down was half the size of a tun barrel and was known as a pipe or a butt. This usually held 126 wine gallons or 1,008 pints. Probably the most famous story about a wine butt is that in 1478 Edward IV's brother, the Duke of Clarence, was reported to have drowned in a butt of malmsey (a sweet Madeira wine). Whether this was a bizarre accident or a euphemism for drinking oneself to death, scholars disagree, but what the story does give us is a mental picture of a wine butt that is large enough to fit a man inside. The next barrel in size was a puncheon or tertian, which was one-third the size of a tun at *c.*84 wine gallons. It is thought that it became known as a puncheon because the wooden barrels would have been marked using a punch. Its alternative name of tertian means 'one-third' in Latin. The wine hogshead was the next size down and is a quarter of a tun at 63 wine gallons. It is not known where this barrel got its porcine name from. Certainly other northern European languages use a similar animal-based word to describe wine barrels – *okshoofd* in Dutch and *Oxhoft* in German – but it is unclear why in Britain the animal switched from an ox to a hog. Some etymologists suggest that the name arose from a pig's head mark being applied to the barrels to denote the size, but the reason why this symbol was chosen has been lost. A tierce is the following size of wine cask, traditionally holding 42 wine gallons or one-sixth of a tun or half a puncheon. Notably a traditional barrel of oil is the same size as a wine tierce, at 42 US gallons. Tierce barrels were the size most frequently used to ship various commodities, including eel, salmon, molasses, whale oil and, of course, wine to the American colonies in the early eighteenth century. The wine barrel comes next, at ⅛ of a tun or half a hogshead. And last but not least was the smallest wine cask, the rundlet, which was ¼₄ of a tun or 18 wine gallons.

This system of wine casks, each of which was easily divisible by the others, was used to transport and keep wine until the advent of the metric system. The American and Britain systems were initially in accordance because the US gallon is based on the

Britain wine gallon of 231 cubic inches set by Queen Anne in 1707. However, on the introduction of the imperial system in 1824 the tun was redefined in Britain as 210 imperial gallons, causing the two systems to diverge.

Today, after the development of cheap, light and durable plastic and metal barrels, wine is no longer traditionally transported in wooden casks. However, maturing wine in oak barrels (or using oak chips in metal barrels) is still the norm for many varieties, as the oak imparts depth of flavour. The problem with wooden wine casks is that wood is permeable. While some oxygen is beneficial to the ageing and flavour of wine, too much can be detrimental. To counteract the risk of oxidation wine would be transported in large barrels (usually a tun) and then, once it reached its destination, it could be decanted into smaller barrels for storage.

By the seventeenth century technology had allowed the development of the glass wine bottle. This allowed wine to be transported in small but robust bottles stopped with a cork. Glass bottles prevented so much air getting to the wine, meaning that the contents stayed drinkable for longer. So they quickly became the favoured container for storing wine. The earliest wine bottles had fat bottoms and short necks and were individually blown. The size of these bottles was determined by the size of an average man's lungs because they were blown by glass-blowers in one continuous lungful, and usually came up as between 700 and 800 ml. This meant, however, that they were considered unreliable as a measure because each bottle differed slightly. Over time the shape of the bottles was lengthened and made streamlined, because when bottles are laid on their sides the cork is kept wet, keeping the seal airtight for longer and preventing the wine from spoiling. By around the 1820s recognizably modern wine bottle shapes had come into use. Also at this time the first factories began producing standard-sized wine bottles, meaning that every bottle was the same size.

Despite the development of wine bottles it was actually illegal in Britain to sell wine in bottles from 1636 up until 1860. This was because it was thought that untrustworthy wine merchants might water down or adulterate the wine if it was sold in such small quantities. To get around this the wealthy would have their own collection of wine bottles that they would send out to their vintner, who would decant their casks of wine into them and send them back. Because wine kept better in bottles it became increasingly common to deliberately age bottles of wine to improve the flavour. This helped to popularize the wine bottle. Wine bottles varied in size until the 1970s, when Europe and America agreed on a standard 750 ml or 75 cl bottle to make it easier to

Tun	*c.* 954 litres	252 wine gallons
Pipe or butt	*c.* 477 litres	126 wine gallons
Puncheon or tertian	*c.* 318 litres	84 wine gallons
Wine hogshead	*c.* 238 litres	63 wine gallons
Tierce	*c.* 159 litres	42 wine gallons
Wine barrel	*c.* 118 litres	31.5 wine gallons
Rundlet	*c.* 68 litres	18 wine gallons

charge import/export duty. It seems likely that the 75 cl size was chosen as the size of a standard bottle blown in one lungful of air.

Research published in the *British Medical Journal* in 2017 suggests that the size of wine glasses have grown sevenfold since 1700. Researchers from Cambridge University looked at historical wine glasses and discovered that an average wine glass was 66 ml in the 1700s, whereas today the average wine glass is 449 ml. As larger wine glasses have become more popular so too has the average wine measure increased. In British pubs today wine is served in 125 ml, 175 ml and 250 ml measures, reflecting the 'go large' trend which has served to normalize increasingly oversized portions of food and drink. According to the NHS a large glass (250 ml) of red, white or rosé wine at 12 per cent ABV, representing a third of a bottle of wine, is equivalent to three units of alcohol.

Ale measures

The importance of ale in British culture is demonstrated by the fact that, like wine, it had its own specific set of measures. The traditional ale gallon was the largest gallon at 282 cubic inches; it was on the basis of this measure that all other ale measures, from casks to pints, were related. The art of brewing developed in monasteries; in Britain the monks would make enough beer for the communities they served. However, as demand for beer increased it began to be traded further and further afield, necessitating a practical method of storage and transportation. Wooden barrels were the most obvious solution and they were often lined with materials such as pitch in order to render them as watertight as possible. By the medieval period the most common size of ale cask was the 'barrel', which at that time was equivalent to 32 imperial gallons or 145.5 litres. Due to its ubiquity all ale casks came to be colloquially known as 'barrels' despite the fact that other cask sizes had their own distinct names and measures within the brewing industry. When the imperial system was adopted in 1824 the barrel was redefined as 36 imperial gallons. The ale hogshead was larger than a barrel. Although the measurement differed (indeed in England from the mid-fifteenth century until 1854 an ale hogshead and a beer hogshead were different sizes) from 48 to 54 ale gallons, it was finally standardized in 1824 as 54 imperial gallons for beer. The size below a barrel is known as a kilderkin, which comes from the Dutch for 'small cask'. The size of a kilderkin varied between 16 and 18 gallons but was set at 18 imperial gallons in 1824, which makes it half the size of a barrel. The firkin is half the size of a kilderkin at 9 imperial gallons and is the traditional size used to transport cask ales. Most British pubs serving cask ales will have them delivered in firkins. The name 'firkin' comes from the Middle Dutch *vierdekijn*, which means 'fourth', revealing its traditional relationship to the barrel. The smallest beer or ale cask is known as a 'pin' and is half the size of a firkin, holding 4.5 imperial gallons. Since the explosion in the popularity of 'real ale' and micro-breweries a modern version of the pin has been introduced known as the 'polypin'. This is a 36-pint container made from plastic, with an integral tap, held inside a cardboard box. These modern pins are made for parties or festivals and can be ordered direct from breweries.

In the 1950s wooden beer casks began to be replaced by steel equivalents. The new steel casks were still made in the traditional sizes so that they would seem interchangeable with their wooden predecessors. Steel casks had the advantage of being much lighter than wooden casks, and this was improved on when aluminium alloy casks were introduced in the 1960s. These days beers and ciders are usually transported in metal kegs. A keg is not an official unit of measurement, so shapes and sizes differ according to the contents, brewer or country. Most British pubs use kegs with the capacity of a firkin (72 pints or 9 imperial gallons), whereas in America most beer kegs are about 15.5 US gallons.

BEER BARRELS

Hogshead	54 imperial gallons	432 pints
Barrel	36 imperial gallons	288 pints
Kilderkin	18 imperial gallons	144 pints
Firkin	9 imperial gallons	72 pints
Pin	4.5 imperial gallons	36 pints

Champagne bottle sizes

When we think of oversized wine bottles we usually think of magnums of champagne, but large-capacity wine bottles were actually first developed in Bordeaux for still wine. As bottle-making technology improved it was noted that wines aged more successfully in a glass bottle. Winemakers soon discovered that larger bottles enabled the wine to age more slowly and therefore to develop more nuanced flavours, and so in Bordeaux they began using magnums. These large-size wine bottles looked especially impressive on the dinner table and so became a novelty item to impress guests. From the early twentieth century champagne producers began to custom-make larger bottles for their favoured clients to display and drink at parties and celebrations. No one is quite sure why biblical kings were chosen as the naming theme and the kings selected are not in logical chronological order. Instead it seems likely that the theme was chosen to link champagne to powerful ancient royalty. A standard champagne bottle is 75 cl and is known as a champenoise. These bottles hold six glasses of champagne. The thick glass is gently sloped down to the base, which has a special concave bottom known as a 'punt'. The punt increases the strength of the bottle and helps it to resist the pressure from the gas within. It also offers a handy place to put your thumb when pouring from the bottle. Magnums are double the size of a standard bottle, holding 1.5 litres. The name comes from the Latin for 'great'. Magnums are known as the best size for ageing vintage champagnes because their size means they have a lower ratio of gas to liquid, which helps the wine to age more gradually. Jeroboams are double magnums at 3 litres, holding 24 glasses of champagne. Jeroboam I was a tenth-century BCE king of Israel; it is thought these extra-large bottles were named in his honour. The sizes after jeroboam are increasingly rare as they are generally only made by champagne producers on request for particularly large events. The re-hoboam, at 4.5 litres of champagne, is named after the son of King Solomon, Rehoboam, who ruled the Kingdom of Judah in the tenth century BCE. According to the Hebrew Bible, Methuselah was the oldest person to ever live; it is after this ancient character that the 6 litre (48 glasses) bottle is named. The salmanazar (9 litres; 72 glasses) is named after an Assyrian king who conquered the Kingdom of Israel in the eighth century BCE. The balthazar (12 litres; 96 glasses) is thought to be named after the Arabian monarch who later became one of the three kings that delivered a gift of myrrh to the baby Jesus. The nebuchadnezzar (15 litres; 120 glasses) is likely named after Nebuchadnezzar II, Babylon's greatest ruler. The solomon (18 litres; 144 glasses) is named after Rehoboam's father and the son of King David. Wise King Solomon famously solved a dispute between two mothers by threatening to chop a baby in half (but I'm not sure anyone would feel that wise after quaffing 144 glasses of champagne). For PR purposes some champagne houses have occasionally produced even larger bottles of champagne, but the impracticality of actually pouring anything out of them makes them more of a novelty factor than a functional wine bottle.

Bottle	Magnum	Jeroboam	Rehoboam	Methuselah
0.75L	1.5L	3L	4.5L	6L

CLAYTON, SHUTTLEWORTH, & CO'S.

NINE HORSE POWER DOUBLE CYLINDER

STEAM ENGINE.

Price £255.   Weight, 75 cwt.
Consumption of Coals per day of ten hours, 9 cwt.
Ditto of Water...   ...   .800 gallons.

CULINARY
& INFORMAL
MEASURES

'It is really just as bad technique to make
a measurement more accurately than is
necessary as it is to make it not accurately
enough.'

ARTHUR DAVID RITCHIE

Smidgen, pinch, dollop, dash & drop

These words, used casually in a recipe, fill novice cooks with fear. Most people recognize that they refer to a small amount of something, but just how small is left open to interpretation. When recipes first began to be written down they were recorded in the vernacular, rather than with a rigid list of exact measurements, meaning that many recipes are peppered with these inexact terms. Some delightful examples of imprecise cooking measurements are seen in *Martha Lloyd's Household Book*, written in the eighteenth century and recently published in facsimile: 'Fricassee Turnips: Cut your Turnips in dice, when boiled and put a little cream to them, Thickened with flour & add a little lump of sugar to your taste.' As recipe-writing has become more standardized (and weighing scales more reliable) most weights and measures are given in official measures. However, for seasoning we have kept many of the traditional words, such as 'smidgen', 'pinch' and 'dash', which I like to think gives the cook room to adjust the amount to their personal taste.

'Smidgen' likely comes from the Scottish word *smitch*, which also means a very small amount. (A side note: it is interesting that many words for small quantities start with 'sm' – including the word 'small' itself; for example, 'smithereen', 'smattering', 'smudge'.) 'Smidgen' is generally used to refer to an almost trace amount, a few grains or a tiny sliver. A 'pinch' is more obvious as it relates to how much you can hold between index finger and thumb. It perfectly encapsulates the physical act of taking a small amount of seasoning and throwing it into the pan. 'Dash' and 'drop' both tend to relate to liquid, and again they conjure up a mental image of the correct amount – a single drop of liquid falling from a spout or the verve of a sudden shake of a bottle which results in a larger dash. 'Dollop' means a lump or clump and comes from 'dallop', the East Anglian dialect word meaning a 'tuft of grass'. Dollop generally refers to something viscous, such as cream, mayonnaise or yoghurt. It has a glorious onomatopoeic character which readily conjures up the sound of a blob of cream plopping luxuriously from spoon to plate.

To assist novice cooks it seems some American food writers have begun giving exact measurements (as fractions of teaspoons) to the traditionally in-exact terms. A dash is said to be ⅛ of a teaspoon, a pinch ¹⁄₁₆ of a teaspoon, a smidgen ¹⁄₃₂ of a teaspoon, and a drop ¹⁄₆₄ of a teaspoon. You can now even purchase a set of measuring spoons for these tiny amounts. I have noted them here for posterity, but it is perhaps best to keep them undefined. I see them as the element of the recipe that grants me licence to add as much or as little as I see fit, so my dash might be rather sparing when it is vinegar but tends to get rather more expansive when it is wine.

✖ General Hints ✖

HANDY MEASURES

1 tablespoonful flour (as much above the rim of the spoon as below)	= 1 oz.
1 level tablespoonful castor sugar	= ½ oz.
1 tablespoonful jam, honey or syrup	= 2 oz.
7 tablespoonfuls water	= ¼ pint
1 gill	= ¼ pint
1 breakfast cup flour (holding ½ pint liquid)	= approximately 4–5 oz.
1 breakfast cup castor sugar (holding ½ pint liquid)	= ½ lb.
1 hen's egg weighs about	= 2 oz.
1 hen's egg	= 2 tablespoonfuls of liquid
A piece of butter, lard or margarine the size of a small egg	= 1 oz.
3 pennies	= 1 oz.
1 penny and 1 halfpenny	= ½ oz.

Teaspoon & tablespoon

The spoon was one of the earliest utensils used by humans. A seashell or scoop-shaped stone could easily be adopted as a means to convey food from plate to mouth. Archaeological evidence suggests it was the Ancient Egyptians in around 1000 BCE who first added a handle to the spoon, the shape of which mimicked that of a scooped palm. These early spoons, made from wood, bone or ivory, were likely used for ceremonial purposes rather than everyday eating. The Romans and Greeks began making spoons in metals such as bronze and silver, their high value meaning they were reserved for the upper classes and as such a status symbol.

By the medieval period across Europe spoons were used as eating utensils by all strata of society and were fashioned from wood, horn or pewter. Metal spoons were still largely reserved for the upper classes; the first mention of a spoon in English historical sources comes from 1259 when silver spoons were cited in the will of Martin of St Cross, master of Sherburn Hospital, Durham. From the Tudor period a set of small silver spoons known as 'Apostle spoons' became a popular christening gift, attesting to the enduring value and utility of a set of spoons. Apostle spoons came in sets of twelve, with the Apostles featured on the top. Some sets came with a thirteenth 'master spoon' depicting Christ. Wealthy families could afford to gift a whole set, but those of more modest means might purchase a smaller set, such as the four evangelists. This began the tradition across Europe of gifting silver spoons on the occasion of major life events, such as a christening or wedding present. Silver spoons held their value and could be sold in times of need, an aspect that hasn't changed. (Indeed, in the 1960s when my parents were students at Oxford and wanted to get married they sold a silver spoon in order to purchase wedding rings.)

The spoons mentioned so far came in all sorts of shapes and sizes and were considered either useful utensils or precious heirlooms. Most people carried their own spoons around with them, much as today you might carry your phone and keys. But by the 1700s things began to change as table settings came into fashion: utensils and crockery laid out neatly ready for the diners to use. This new fashion meant that people did not need to carry their own spoon around with them anymore, but it also led to a whole flurry of new implements – table forks, table knives, tablespoons, dessert spoons – covering a whole range of dishes. The tablespoon was a large spoon used for serving. Its handy size meant that by the 1800s it became unofficially adopted as part of the apothecaries' system as a unit of measure. In America the tablespoon measure was 4 fluid drams, which was equivalent to 3 teaspoons or 14.8 ml, whereas in the United Kingdom the tablespoon was given as 15 ml (but also 3 teaspoons). Australia, however, threw another spoon measurement into the mix, classifying a tablespoon as 20 ml, which apparently is equivalent to 2 dessert spoons or 4 teaspoons.

At around the same time that place settings were becoming a custom, specific teaspoons began to be used because tea had become a popular beverage in Europe. The first teaspoons were smaller than we would expect today and were more like paddles than scoops, as their main function was to stir milk and sugar into a cup of tea. In the 1700s tea was very expensive (subject to taxes of up to 114 per cent), and so both teacups and teaspoons were small in size, allowing each sip to be savoured. It was not until the mid-nineteenth century that the taxes on tea were reduced and it became a more affordable commodity. Cheaper tea meant bigger cups and bigger spoons, and so at this point teaspoons began to resemble the spoons we use today. Around the same time standardization of medical measures became more important as doctors and pharmacists became increasingly professionalized. As a result the unofficial apothecaries' measure of a 'teaspoon' was set as 1 fluid dram (5 ml today).

Up until the late nineteenth century standardized culinary measurement was unknown, most recipes being passed down verbally with approximations (for example, 'a good amount of flour' or 'a piece of butter the size of an egg'). Cheaper machine-made utensils increased the standardization of teaspoons and tablespoons, making them a good choice for small measures in cooking; after all, not everyone had a set of weighing scales but most people had some spoons. Thus when more scientific and accurate measures began to be given with recipes, by trailblazers such as the American Fannie Farmer, who published *The Boston Cooking-School Cook Book* in 1896, teaspoons and tablespoons were adopted as small measures for dry and wet goods. Farmer became known as 'the mother of level measurements' and her scientific approach to recipe-writing was very influential. Anyone could pick up her book and follow an exact recipe to ensure a cake or pastry would turn out as Farmer intended. The teaspoon (commonly abbreviated to 'tsp') thus became set as a standard 5 ml, meaning that there are three teaspoons in every tablespoon (commonly abbreviated to 'tbsp'). However, it is not all plain sailing: a measure of personal judgement is required when deciding the exact amount in a teaspoon or tablespoon. In theory when a recipe calls for 1 tsp or 1 tbsp the measure should be scraped flat to the bowl of the spoon with a knife. The complication comes when a rounded or heaped spoon is called for. This measurement has no exact value and instead allows the cook to decide just how precipitously they wish to stack their spoon.

Cup

Europeans often puzzle at the American cup measurement, which is used in recipes for both wet and dry measurements. In Europe most wet measurements are given in millilitres (or pints in Britain) while dry measures are given in grams or ounces. The cup, however, is a measure of volume rather than weight and it is traditionally given as half a liquid pint, which, somewhat inevitably, differs in measurement between America and Britain. In America a 'liquid pint' is 473 ml and in Britain the imperial pint is 568 ml (see page 108). There is no definitive answer as to why Americans use the volume measure of cup in their recipes, but one of the most credible explanations involves the history of the weighing scale and the relative poverty of eighteenth-century Americans.

Before the invention of the spring scale in the 1770s most objects were weighed using a balance scale. The earliest balance scales date back to 2000 BCE and were found in the Indus Valley region of modern-day Pakistan. Balance scales work by having two plates attached to a horizontal pole, which is itself attached to a central pole on a pivot. The item to be weighed is placed on one side and then small weights are added to the other side until they balance and are therefore of equal weight. This technology stayed roughly the same for thousands of years until in the 1770s British spring-maker Richard Salter developed the spring weight. This innovation revealed the weight of an object through a measurement of the tension on a spring. The spring scale was much more accurate than the balance scale, but its introduction came at a tumultuous time in American history.

A balance scale was a cumbersome item requiring numerous counterweights, meaning that it was not an easily portable piece of equipment. This factor would have surely made early European settlers in America unlikely to want to lug such a heavy scale around. The invention of the spring scale in the 1770s coincided with the American Revolution (1775–83), and this may have influenced its delayed adoption. Similarly the hardships of life on the American frontier likely also caused the rejection of too many fiddly bits of equipment – why cart about a heavy balance scale or an expensive spring scale when you could just have an all-purpose cup of a regular size with which to make measurements? Most people owned a cup already and it made sense to use this same item to scoop up a measure of flour or sugar when baking. On balance it seems likely that the ease of measuring with a regular-sized cup was one of the reasons why this measurement was so widely adopted across the United States. Although the spring scale and, more recently, the digital weighing scale are both now used in America, the traditional method of measuring dry and wet goods with cups has persisted and it is still the most frequently used in American recipes.

1 TBSP 1 TSP 1/2 TSP
1/4 TSP 1/8 TSP 1/16 TSP
1/2 TBSP 1 CUP 3/4 CUP
1/2CUP 1/3 CUP 1/4 CUP 1/8 CUP

Alcohol proof

Alcohol proof was developed in sixteenth-century England as a way to tax spirits. In this context 'proof' means a 'test' or 'trial' to reveal if the alcohol content was sufficiently high for the beverage to be subject to a higher tax level – a level which was set at the arbitrary value of 100 proof. To determine the level of proof, a pellet of gunpowder was soaked in the liquor in question and then set alight. If it burned it was considered 'proof' that the spirit should be taxed; if it did not it was classed as 'under proof' and therefore not subject to a higher level of tax. This method of testing liquor was notoriously inaccurate as the flammability of alcohol is temperature-dependent, meaning that the temperature of the air or of the liquid itself could unduly influence the likelihood of ignition.

A test with greater accuracy was introduced in England towards the end of the seventeenth century. This new test was based on specific gravity, which is the ratio of the density of alcohol to the density of water. This method was refined over many years. In 1816 the proof of alcohol was officially fixed in Britain at an alcohol level $\frac{12}{13}$ the weight of an equal volume of distilled water at the same temperature. Today the standard worldwide measure for the strength of alcohol is alcohol by volume (ABV), which reveals how much ethanol (pure alcohol) is contained in a specific volume of alcoholic beverage. ABV is usually expressed as a percentage. Proof is fixed in Britain at the gravity $^{12}/_{13}$ of water and is the equivalent of 57.15 per cent ABV. The figure of $^4/_7$ = 0.5714 is almost the value of proof expressed as ABV. To work out the proof of a liquor from the ABV it was generally multiplied by $^7/_4$ (which is equivalent to $1\frac{3}{4}$). A spirit with an ABV of 50 per cent would therefore have a proof of 87.5 ($50 \times \frac{7}{4}$).

The system in America developed quite differently, although Americans adopted the British way of describing the alcohol level as 'proof'. By 1848 in America the standard measure for alcohol content was measured using percentage rather than specific gravity. This was a much simpler and easier-to-understand system which classed 100 proof as 50 per cent ABV, meaning that the 'proof' of alcohol was always double the ABV. Although proof is still occasionally used, most bottles of alcohol in America now show alcohol content with ABV, like in the rest of the world.

A third method of measuring proof and the most straightforward was developed in France in 1824 by the celebrated chemist Joseph-Louis Gay-Lussac. In his system 100 per cent alcohol by volume is classed as 100 proof, whereas 100 per cent water by volume is 0 proof. This makes the proof number and the ABV exactly the same. To highlight the differences in the three systems we can consider a typical Scotch whisky with an ABV of 40 per cent in Britain, which would be 70° proof. In America this would be 80° proof. In France it would be 40° proof. Thankfully this divergence in systems has been largely nullified by the worldwide adoption of ABV as a more accurate method to show the strength of alcohol.

Baker's dozen

Order a dozen apples from the greengrocer and you'd expect to get twelve apples. Order a dozen envelopes from the stationer and you'd expect to get twelve envelopes. However, if you ordered a dozen bread rolls from the baker's you'd expect to receive thirteen rolls as it has become commonly accepted that a baker's dozen is equivalent to thirteen. The reason for this strange anomaly has never been conclusively proven but the most likely explanation has its roots in English laws imposed to regulate the sale of bread. As a vital foodstuff the selling of loaves of bread which were underweight was seen as a serious breach of trust and in around 1260 Henry III introduced a law to protect consumers from un-scrupulous traders. The Assize of Bread and Ale statute set out the relationship between the price of wheat and the price of a loaf of bread made from a certain quantity of that wheat, effectively setting the expected weight of a penny loaf. This meant that any baker selling bread under the expected weight could be punished. This became fraught with difficulty for bakers because at that time they did not have the technology to accurately weigh out ingredients, and such is the alchemy of bread-making that it can be difficult to achieve standard loaves every time.

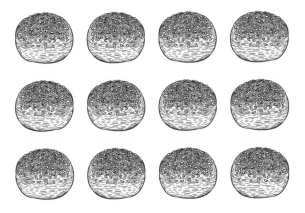

To mitigate against this problem, when selling a dozen rolls or loaves of bread bakers would add an extra roll or loaf at no extra cost, meaning that the customer got thirteen for the price of twelve. This meant they could be confident that they were getting the weight of bread they requested. This extra thirteenth loaf became known as 'in-bread' and was seen as a sensible free addition by the bakers to make sure they did not sell underweight bread and to keep them on the right side of the law.

An alternative explanation has been offered which may have contributed to the adoption of the informal measurement. When bakers sold large numbers of loaves to street vendors or middlemen they would throw in some in-bread with every dozen. This meant that the vendor would sell on all thirteen loaves at full price and keep all of the value of the thirteenth loaf as their profit. This allowed the baker, in the role of a wholesaler, to get full value for twelve rolls and to get round the rules of the Assize of Bread and Ale which prevented them from selling their wares at a cheaper price to vendors. In this way the practice of adding a thirteenth in-bread to every dozen became customary and was adopted as standard by London's Worshipful Company of Bakers, further cementing the practice. Today, however, the baker's dozen lives on mostly in idiom rather than in practice – if you buy a dozen rolls from a supermarket you will receive just twelve rolls.

Carats & karats

Simply put, carats are used to measure the weight of gemstones such as diamonds, whereas karats are a measure of the purity of gold. In the UK 'carat' is used for both types of measure, but for the purposes of clarity in this entry I will use 'carats' for diamond weight and 'karats' (the American spelling) for gold purity.

The word 'carat' comes from the Greek word *kerátion*, which means 'carob seed'. This is because in the ancient world it was believed that carob seeds all weighed the same and so were frequently used to measure small quantities, much as barleycorns were used in Britain (see page 48). The word entered Arabic as *qirat* and then began appearing in fourteenth-century France as *carat*, where it was was used as a measure of the fineness of gold. From France the word and concept spread to England.

Karat as a measure of the fineness of gold came first. The Romans named a small silver coin the *siliqua*, so called because of the measurement based on carob seeds the *siliqua graeca*; 24 of these coins were equivalent to 1 solidus, which was both a pure gold coin and a unit of weight. Therefore 1 solidus comprised 24 karats, thereby setting 24 karats as pure gold. The karat became the standard way of expressing the weight of gold. However, the exact weight of a karat differed from country to country and it was not until 1907 that a standard metric karat was agreed to be 200 milligrams. In 1873 the Germans introduced the coin known as the 'mark', which weighed 24 karats. But because gold is quite soft it needs to be combined with other metals, such as copper, to make it hard enough to be a durable coin. As a result karats in this context were no longer used as a measure of weight but began to be associated with the purity of the gold. For example, if a coin was made from 18 parts gold and 6 parts copper it would be classed as 18 karat gold, and if it was 20 parts gold and 4 parts copper it would be 20 karat gold.

The carat has the same root as the karat and was initially equivalent to the Ancient Greek carob seed weight. By the 1570s gemstone traders and diamond merchants began using the weight to describe their jewels, although each country tended to have its own definition of carat weight. For example, in 1888 the British Board of Trade defined the carat as 3.168 grains (205 grams), whereas in Venice it was 207 grams. Since 1907 the carat has been internationally agreed to weigh 200 grams. Diamonds are usually given as decimals; for example, an average diamond for an engagement ring might be described as 0.6 carats (which would weigh 0.12 grams).

The largest cut fine-quality colourless diamond in the world is Cullinan I, which is 530 carats. It was cut from an enormous raw diamond discovered in South Africa in 1905 which weighed 3,106 carats – the largest ever found. It was cut into nine large diamonds and about 100 smaller ones by expert jeweller Joseph Asscher, who reportedly fainted with nervous exhaustion after making the cut. Cullinan I, II and III are all now part of the English Crown jewels.

Horsepower

Today 'horsepower' is used to describe the power of an engine, so if you were buying a ride-on mower, a chainsaw or a sports car you might see its capabilities described in terms of horsepower. But where did this measurement come from? The first commercially available steam engines were invented by Thomas Newcomen in 1712 but they were fairly inefficient. Scottish inventor James Watt came up with an improved version in 1763 which used a condensation chamber to reduce inefficient heat loss. This innovation made the steam engine a much more viable product and Watt began to sell them as an alternative to dray horses. However, he needed a good marketing hook to convince people to move away from actual horses and towards technology.

At the dawn of the Industrial Revolution most pulling power came from huge dray horses: they transported goods and ploughed fields. In order to show people that one engine could do the work of many horses, Watt came up with the idea to create a measurement of 'horsepower'. This, he hoped, would allow him to prove the enhanced pulling power of his steam engine. Watt used his observation of Welsh pit ponies, which pulled coal up mineshafts, to estimate how much a larger dray horse might be able to pull. A pit pony could drag a single cart filled with 220 lb of coal 100 feet up a mineshaft in the space of one minute, which gives 22,000 lb-ft per minute. As dray horses were substantially larger than pit ponies, Watt wrongly assumed that they would produce at least 50 per cent more power, so he set the unit of horsepower at 33,000 lb-ft per minute. (Recent research has shown that large horses are actually only marginally stronger than the small but stocky Shetland ponies used in the mines, achieving approximately 0.7 horsepower.)

The fact that Watt overestimated the power of a horse actually worked to his advantage as it meant his steam-powered engines always easily outperformed horsepower. Once Watt had set horsepower at 33,000 lb-ft per minute he was able to directly compare his machines to horses, and by saying that his steam engine had '10 horsepower' and therefore could do the 'work' of ten horses he was able to convince many farmers, mine owners and hauliers to invest in a steam engine. Horsepower became such a successful way to show the pulling ability of a steam engine that Watt's competitors also began to use the measure. As technology improved and new types of mechanical and steam engines were developed it remained in use as the standard description of power.

Quire, ream, bundle & bale

The first 'books' were made of papyrus and came in the form of a scroll. Papyrus was used in Ancient Egypt, pre-dating the invention of actual paper in China, and is the root of the English word 'paper'. Made from *Cyperus papyrus*, it was fashioned from strips of pith laid side by side and pummelled into a sheet. A further sheet was then laid on top at right angles and again pounded to form one very strong sheet of papyrus. In China paper made from tree fibres was said to have been invented in 105 CE by Cai Lun, an imperial eunuch of the Han dynasty (206 BCE–220 CE). Archaeological evidence, however, reveals fragments of Chinese paper from as early as the third century BCE. Paper technology was thought to have reached the Islamic world by the eighth century CE, with evidence of papermaking occurring at Samarkand in modern-day Uzbekistan. Scholars disagree on whether the Islamic world developed its own papermaking techniques or if it learned them from the Chinese, but at this time most paper made in China was formed from plant fibre, whereas early Islamic paper was largely made out of waste materials such as rags. From the Islamic world paper made its way to the Middle East, from where it would finally arrive in Europe in the twelfth century.

Before this point in Europe vellum or parchment, formed of animal skins, was used in place of paper. From the second century BCE parchment or papyrus scrolls began to be replaced by early books in codex format. They were formed by folding sheets of papyrus or parchment into quires, which were traditionally four sheets of parchment folded to form eight leaves. This original definition of a 'quire' is where we get the word from, as it derives from the Medieval Latin *quaternum*, meaning 'set of four sheets of parchment or paper'. A typical four-sheet, eight-leaf quire can be fashioned from one large single sheet of parchment folded and then cut at the edges to make a booklet. Parchment was easier to write on and more durable than papyrus so it came to be the favoured material from which to make codices. In Europe early books were fashioned and copied by hand by monks. In these early books quires (also known as 'gatherings') were not standardized and so they ranged in size from two to twenty leaves but were most frequently made from four sheets of parchment which was folded and cut to form a booklet of eight leaves or sixteen sides. Quires could be sewn together to form a larger book with many pages. Traditional book formats were named by how many times the paper was folded to make a quire. So a large book in which the paper is folded only once is known as a folio. When the paper is folded twice it is known as quarto. If it is folded three times it is known as octavo. The names of the book formats come from the number of leaves in the quires used to form them. In this way the volume of a quire depended on which book format was being followed.

From the twelfth century in Europe papermaking technology was introduced from the Middle East, and paper made from plant pulp and rags slowly superseded parchment. The introduction of the printing press increased book production, but quires were still not a standard number of leaves because the quires differed in size depending on the format of the book. These early printed books were not sold as bound objects but rather delivered as quires and bound separately at the cost of the buyer. As paper began to be manufactured in paper mills (the first mill in Britain was Sele Mill near Hertford, which opened in 1488) paper was sold and packaged in quires. These were usually between 20 and 25 sheets. Over time the quire came to be accepted as 24 sheets of paper, and in England this was known as the imperial quire. In America the 24-sheet quire was known as the 'short quire'. The imperial quire is still often used for packaging writing paper; but for most other manufactured paper the metric quire of 25 sheets is now used, which takes its definition from the modern international standard (ISO) of the ream.

A ream is a large bundle of paper, measured by the sheet; the term is used in paper manufacturing. The word 'ream' reflects the introduction of paper into Europe via the Moors in Spain, as it derives from the Arabic word *rizmah*, which means 'a bundle of paper'. This became *resma* in Spanish and then *reyme* in Old French before becoming the English 'ream'. A variety of different reams operated regionally, often depending on the number of sheets in the quires used to make up the reams. In Britain reams were originally 480 sheets, made up of twenty quires of 24 sheets; more recently, as quires became customarily 25 sheets, a ream came to be 500 sheets, or twenty quires of 25 sheets. Additionally a printer's ream of 516 sheets was also used, which made allowances for the wastage caused by printing and handling paper. This ensured the customer would end up with at least 500 usable sheets. In modern times the ream has been officially standardized after being included in the ISO 4046 and DIN 6730 standards on paper and board, which define one ream of 80 gsm A4 paper as being 500 sheets. Two reams of paper are known as a 'bundle' of 1,000 sheets (or 40 quires). A 'bale' of paper is 5,000 sheets or 5 bundles, 10 reams or 200 quires.

SCALES & SCORES

'By measurement to knowledge [*door meten tot weten*] I should like to write as a motto above the entrance to every physics laboratory.'

HEIKE KAMERLINGH ONNES

Beaufort wind scale

Sailors have used unofficial wind scales for hundreds of years to record the weather in a ship's log. The scales were generally based on empirical observations of the state of the water or the effect of the wind on sails. In this way over the years the language used to describe certain sea conditions became relatively standardized. In 1703 a great storm struck central and southern England causing the loss of over 4,000 trees in the New Forest and killing up to 15,000 people as debris flew through the air and chimney stacks crashed to the ground. Novelist Daniel Defoe, who had a keen interest in the weather, in 1704 published *The Storm*, which comprised a series of personal accounts of the cyclone. Through his observations Defoe was inspired to create a wind scale. Defoe's scale had 12 points, which were probably based on the words commonly used by sailors to describe wind speeds. It was as follows:

0	stark calm	6	a top sail gale
1	calm weather	7	blows fresh
2	little wind	8	a hard gale of wind
3	a fine breeze	9	a fret of wind
4	a small gale	10	a storm
5	a fresh gale	11	a tempest

Defoe's scale and a number of similar scales, mostly based on traditional terms used by sailors in their logbooks, continued to be used informally until 1806, when Commander Francis Beaufort developed his 13-point scale. Beaufort was clearly influenced by scales such as that created by Alexander Dalrymple, for use across the East India Company, in which Beaufort served an apprenticeship. The original Beaufort scale was relatively basic; it did not reference actual wind speeds but was based on how winds at sea affected the sails of a fully rigged man-of-war, the main type of ship used by the Royal Navy at that time. The scale stopped at level 12 'hurricane', classed as winds 'which no canvas sails could withstand'.

Beaufort continued to consult on and refine his scale. In 1831 Captain FitzRoy of HMS *Beagle* agreed to use the scale during his five-year voyage. FitzRoy, aside from being a great sailor, also had a keen interest in the weather; in 1854 he formed the Meteorological Department of the Board of Trade, which later became known as the Met Office. By 1838 the Royal Navy had accepted Beaufort's wind scale and decreed that it should be used aboard all Royal Navy ships, cementing its status as the standard wind scale.

Over the years various improvements have been made to the scale; for example, the descriptions of the effects of the wind on land. In the twentieth century several attempts were made to correlate the scale

THE BEAUFORT SCALE ON LAND AND SEA

Force	Knots	Name	For use on land
0	< 1	Calm	Smoke rises vertically.
1	1–3	Light air	Direction of wind shown by smoke drift but not by wind vanes.
2	4–6	Light breeze	Wind felt on face, leaves rustle, ordinary wind vanes moved by wind.
3	7–10	Gentle breeze	Leaves and small twigs in constant motion; wind extends light flags.
4	11–16	Moderate breeze	Wind raises dust and loose paper; small branches move.
5	17–21	Fresh breeze	Small trees in leaf start to sway; crested wavelets on inland waters.
6	22–27	Strong breeze	Large branches in motion; whistling in telegraph wires; umbrellas used with difficulty.
7	28–33	Near gale	Whole trees in motion; inconvenient to walk against the wind.
8	34–40	Gale	Twigs break from trees; difficult to walk.
9	41–47	Strong gale	Slight structural damage occurs; chimney pots and slates removed.
10	48–55	Storm	Trees uprooted; considerable structural damage occurs.
11	56–63	Violent storm	Widespread damage.
12	64	Hurricane	Widespread damage.

Sea like a mirror.

Ripples with the appearance of scales are formed, but without foam crests.

Small wavelets, still short but more pronounced. Crests have a glassy appearance and do not break.

Large wavelets. Crests begin to break. Foam of glassy appearance. Perhaps scattered white horses.

Small waves, becoming longer, fairly frequent white horses.

Moderate waves, taking a more pronounced form; many white horses are formed. Chance of some spray.

Large waves begin to form; the white foam crests are more extensive everywhere. Probably some spray.

Sea heaps up and white foam from breaking waves begins to be blown in streaks along the direction of the wind.

Moderately high waves of greater length; edges of crests begin to break into spindrift. The foam is blown in well-marked streaks along the direction of the wind

High waves. Dense streaks of foam along the direction of the wind. Crests of waves begin to topple, tumble and roll over. Spray may affect visibility.

Very high waves with long overhanging crests. The resulting foam in great patches is blown in dense white streaks along the direction of the wind. On the whole, the surface of the sea takes on a white appearance. The 'tumbling' of the sea becomes heavy and shock-like. Visibility affected.

Exceptionally high waves (small and medium-sized ships might be lost for a time behind the waves). The sea is completely covered with long white patches of foam lying along the direction of the wind. Everywhere the edges of the waves are blown into froth. Visibility affected.

The air is filled with foam and spray, the sea completely white with driving spray. Visibility very seriously affected.

with a measure of wind speed as taken by an anemometer (a measuring device using cups on a propeller to drive an electric generator). After various false starts, in 1939 the International Meteorological Committee adopted a correlated measure of wind speeds taken from an anemometer on a 6-metre pole. In 1955 the Beaufort scale was extended to 17 points to account for typhoons, but the numbers 13 to 17 are generally only used in typhoon-affected areas such as East Asia. For most sailors the 13-point scale suffices, as once 12 has been reached the sea is no longer navigable.

The modern Beaufort scale with wind speeds, observations of sea and land effects is shown on the previous spread. Today most weather services around the world use wind speeds measured in knots (nautical miles per hour) and only shipping forecasts still give a number on the Beaufort scale. In the United Kingdom a 'small craft warning' is given if winds of force 6 are expected up to 10 nautical miles offshore, and levels of 'gale force' warning are given if it is 8 or over on the Beaufort scale. In America 6 or 7 on the Beaufort scale results in a 'small craft advisory' and 10 or 11 is a 'storm warning'. Although wind speeds are now most often expressed in knots, what the Beaufort scale reminds us is that it is not necessarily the speed of the wind which is of concern to us, but the effects of that wind on sea and land.

The Glasgow Coma Scale

The Glasgow Coma Scale (GCS) was developed by neurosurgeons Graham Teasdale and Bryan Jennett as a means to assess a person's level of consciousness after a head trauma. The scale emerged from their work at the Institute of Neurological Sciences, Glasgow, a world-leading research centre on brain trauma. Its purpose was to provide an objective measure of consciousness which could be taken periodically over time, allowing doctors to assess if the patient was progressing or deteriorating. Years of research and observations were brought together by Teasdale and Jennett to create the scale, which was first published in 1974 in the medical journal *The Lancet.* Although it was greeted with enthusiasm on publication it did not gain traction as clinical practice until the 1980s, when it was included in an influential medical text book *Advanced Trauma and Life Support.*

The scale is measured on three types of response to stimulus: the response of the eye, a verbal response and a physical response. Each of the three sectors has its own score, which can then be added together to give an overall GCS number. The lowest score of 3 would mean deep coma or death; the highest score of 15 would mean the patient was fully awake. When the scale was first created the maximum score was 14, but it was later increased to 15 after it was decided to differentiate between extension and flexion within motor (movement) responses. The Glasgow Coma Scale is measured as follows.

Eye response (E) has four grades, with 1 being the most severe:

1. No response.
2. Eyes open in response to pain.
3. Eyes open in response to sound.
4. Eyes open spontaneously.

Verbal response (V) has five grades, with 1 being the most severe:

1. No verbal response.
2. Makes sounds but no words.
3. Words, but not coherent.
4. Confused.
5. Orientated.

Motor response (M) has six grades, with 1 being the most severe. Motor response is assessed by applying pressure to the nail bed to cause mild pain.

1. No response.
2. Extension (decerebrate posturing, a stiff prone posture) in response to pain.

3. Abnormal flexion (decorticate posturing, a stiff posture with bent arms and clenched fists) in response to pain.
4. Normal flexion (pulls hand away from pain).
5. Localizing (purposeful movements away from pain).
6. Obeys commands for movement.

The best score observed in the patient is given for each sector and then added together to give an overall score, which might look like E3, V4, M5, giving an overall score of 12. A score of 8 or less would indicate a severe brain injury, a score of 8 to 12 would be considered moderate, and a score of 13 or more is considered mild. Alcohol or drugs can affect scoring on the GCS, which can result in inaccuracies. A separate scale has also been developed for use with children, as verbal response is not such a good indicator with youngsters. Today the Glasgow Coma Score is used worldwide and is standard in more than eighty countries.

Scoville scale

In 1912 pharmacist Wilbur Scoville created the Scoville Organoleptic Test to rate the heat of chilli peppers. The scale is based on capsaicin, the active component which causes the burning sensation on your tongue. Scoville's method was to extract capsaicin oil from a particular chilli pepper and then dilute it repeatedly in sugar water. The dilution would be given to a panel of five taste-testers who would sip the concoction periodically as it became increasingly dilute until the majority could no longer ascertain any heat from the pepper. Once no heat can be detected a score as a Scoville Heat Unit (SHU) can be assigned based on the level of dilution. For example, if a pepper had to be diluted 10,000 times before its heat was undetectable, then that would give it a score of 10,000 SHU. The higher the score, the hotter the chilli. In the past several years there has been an explosion of interest in developing ever hotter chilli peppers. At the time of writing the hottest pepper in the world according to *The Guinness Book of World Records* is the Carolina Reaper, which was developed by (the appropriately named) Ed Currie. The Carolina Reaper is a hybrid of a ghost pepper and a habanero. It is red in colour, bumpy in texture and is shaped like a scotch bonnet pepper but with a pointed tail. The average SHU for the Carolina Reaper is 1,641,183 SHU, although one individual pepper scored as high as 2.2 million SHU. It has been described as akin to eating molten lava. Below are some notable peppers and their scores on the Scoville scale:

0	Bell peppers
1000–1,500	Poblano chilli
2,500–5,000	Tabasco sauce
2,500–8,000	Jalapeño
30,000–50,000	Cayenne
50,000–100,000	Bird's eye chilli
1,300,000	Naga viper
1,600,000	Carolina reaper
2,000,000–5,300,000	Police pepper spray
16,000,000	Capsaicin
15,000,000,000	Resiniferatoxin (the hottest chemical in the world, found in resin spurge, a cactus-like plant in Morocco)

The Scoville scale is notoriously subjective as it relies on personal taste. Equally it can vary quite dramatically from one chilli to another within the same variety, depending on the growing conditions the chilli enjoyed. As a result, today most heat testing is actually done using high-performance liquid chromatography, which can accurately identify the chemical concentration of capsaicin in any given chilli. However, due to public recognition of the Scoville scale, these scores are usually converted into SHU. For example, in the USA the American Spice Trade Association (ASTA) favours the ASTA Pungency Test, which employs chromatography but is then converted into SHU by multiplying the score by 15.

Richter scale

Most early earthquake scales were based on a subjective visual assessment of the impact of the tremors and relied upon someone close to the epicentre making observations. For example, the 1873 Rossi–Forel scale, which had ten intensity levels, described a 'strong tremor' (number 6 on the scale) as 'General awakening of those asleep. General ringing of bells. Oscillation of chandeliers, stopping of clocks, visible agitation of trees and shrubs. Some startled persons leaving their dwellings.' Subjective scales such as the Rossi–Forel, while charming, were not very scientific and so made it difficult for the intensity of earthquakes to be compared.

By the 1920s understanding of earthquake science had improved. Two scientists, Harry O. Wood and John Anderson, working at the California Institute of Technology (Caltech), developed the Wood–Anderson seismograph, an accurate way to measure seismic waves. To further their research Wood and Anderson installed a network of seismographs across southern California and in 1927 they recruited a young researcher who had just completed his Ph.D. by the name of Charles Richter. Richter's job was to monitor all the seismographs across southern California, record any earthquakes and measure the resultant seismograms. Building on the work of Japanese seismologist Kiyoo Wadati, who showed that the maximum amplitude of an earthquake's seismic waves got smaller with distance at a certain rate, Richter began to use measurements from the seismograms within 100 km of the epicentre of an earthquake to create a scale which could be used to compare the relative size and strength of a quake. Richter was inspired by the stellar magnitude scale used by astronomers, which measures the luminosity (light emitted) of stars. To measure the luminosity of a star, measurements of its brightness are taken which are then adjusted to take account of the magnification of the telescope and the distance from the star. The resulting score is huge, so to make it a more manageable and comparable number, on a smaller scale, astronomers calculate a logarithm (how many times it is multiplied by itself to reach another number) which scales it down into a single-digit number on the stellar magnitude scale. Measurements from seismographs give similarly large numbers and so Richter employed a logarithm, meaning that each step along the scale saw the magnitude of the quake increase tenfold.

In 1935 Richter published the first version of his scale, calling it the 'magnitude scale'. This version was only designed to measure the magnitude of earthquakes which occurred in southern California.

It worked by rating magnitudes by the logarithm of the amplitude of waves recorded by Wood–Anderson seismographs 100 km from the epicentre of the quake. The baseline score of zero was set because a shock at a distance of 100 km produces a maximum amplitude of 1 micron (0.001 mm) on a seismogram as measured with a Wood–Anderson torsion seismograph. Most earthquakes below a score of 3 on the Richter scale are imperceptible to people at the epicentre; therefore quakes scoring below 3 are usually classed as microquakes. The appeal of Richter's scale was that it allowed quakes to be quickly measured from seismographs which did not have to be especially close to the quake, and it could then be easily compared using the resultant single-digit score. A quake of 3 was minor, 6 would cause significant damage, and 9 would produce severe devastation. However, in its early form it only applied to one geographical area (southern California). Richter's colleague Beno Gutenberg therefore adapted the scale so it could be used in any location. Richter also provided a series of correction tables to enable seismographers to measure quakes regardless of the distance between their seismograph and the quake's epicentre.

A new more accurate way of measuring earthquakes had been developed by the late 1970s, known as the moment magnitude scale. This measured the magnitude of the quake through its seismic 'moment', which basically means how much 'work' is done by the faulting of the earthquake. This scale showed much greater accuracy in measuring the size of more powerful quakes and as a result it became the preferred method of measurement for bodies such as the US Geological Survey. Despite Richter's scale having largely been surpassed in the 1970s, its simple scoring method gained popular understanding, so although most people do not understand how the scale works they do understand that an earthquake scoring 6 on the Richter scale is a serious quake. As a result, although most reports of earthquakes now use the moment magnitude scale (which also uses logarithms to allow the score to be given in single digits), reporters often erroneously describe it as the Richter scale. This means that in the popular imagination the Richter scale remains the measure by which we understand the size of earthquakes.

Fujita scale

Tornadoes are enormous tunnels of spinning cloud which reach from thunderclouds to the ground. The majority of tornadoes are relatively weak and short-lived but occasionally a large tornado will gather and this can create some of the highest wind speeds on Earth. Creating a scale to measure tornadoes is especially challenging, because their force means that most gauges designed to measure wind speed would be ripped to shreds. To get round this University of Chicago meteorologist Dr Ted Fujita, working in conjunction with Allen Pearson, head of the National Severe Storms Forecast Center, decided to create a scale to measure the intensity of a tornado which was based on the damage caused to human-built structures and vegetation. By studying previous tornado sites using aerial photographs and eyewitness accounts, the Fujita scale was developed with six levels which pegged estimated wind speeds to levels of damage. It was also designed to tally with the Beaufort scale (see p. 160), a score of F1 on the Fujita scale being equivalent to the highest level of 12 on the Beaufort scale.

Fujita and Pearson's work, which included back-dating scores for all significant tornadoes since 1912, made the scale a significant tool for meteorologists

EF-0

wind speed 105–137 km/hour (65–85 mph)

observations Minor damage to the environment. Tree branches broken, some shallow-rooted trees uprooted, some damage to gutters.

EF-1

wind speed 138–177 km/hour (86–110 mph)

observations Moderate damage to the environment. Mobile homes overturned, windows broken, exterior doors ripped off, some tree trunks snapped.

EF-2

wind speed 178–217 km/hour (111–135 mph)

observations Considerable damage to the environment. Mobile homes destroyed, roofs torn off buildings, cars lifted from the ground.

EF-3

wind speed 218–266 km/hour (136–165 mph)

observations Severe damage to the environment. Roofs and walls ripped off buildings, trains overturned, small buildings destroyed, along with most trees.

EF-4

wind speed 267–322 km/hour (166–200 mph)

observations Devastating damage to the environment. Well-built homes destroyed, cars blown away, large debris flies through the air.

EF-5

wind speed <322 km/hour (over 200 mph)

observations Incredible damage to the environment. Well-built homes lifted from their foundations and blown away, reinforced concrete buildings suffer damage, car-sized debris flies through the air.

working on the phenomenon. However, it was widely accepted that assessing a score was subjective – for example, an inexperienced surveyor might give a tornado a higher score than it merited because all the trees in a park were uprooted, whereas a more experienced surveyor would have noted that the trees were a variety with especially shallow roots. Furthermore, as the scale became more frequently used it became apparent that the estimated wind speeds were higher than the actual speeds required to cause that level of damage. As a result in 2007 the Wind Science and Engineering Research Center at Texas Tech University convened a group of structural engineers and meteorologists to update and refine the scale. This resulted in the 'Enhanced Fujita scale', which uses new wind-speed estimates. The Enhanced Fujita scale is shown on the opposite page.

After a tornado has struck, a team of structural engineers and meteorologists are deployed to assess the damage and assign a score on the Fujita scale. One of the worst tornadoes in recent history hit Joplin, Missouri, in 2011. The mile-wide tornado was rated as EF-5 and saw gusts as high as 200 mph destroy the school and hospital in the city and cause 1,500 vehicles to be thrown into the air.

Bristol stool scale

The Bristol stool scale was developed in 1997 by a team of researchers led by Ken Heaton MD, an expert in bowel function and nutrition, at Bristol Royal Infirmary. The chart was designed to classify seven different types of stool in order to help diagnose gastroenterological problems. To create the scale sixty-six volunteers swallowed radiopaque marker pellets so the transit time through the gut could be measured. The stools were then weighed and details of their consistency recorded in a diary.

BRISTOL STOOL SCALE

TYPE 1	Separate hard lumps (hard to pass)	*Severe constipation*
TYPE 2	Sausage-shaped but lumpy	*Slightly constipated*
TYPE 3	Like a sausage but with cracks on the surface	*Normal*
TYPE 4	Like a sausage or snake, smooth and soft	*Normal*
TYPE 5	Soft blobs with clear-cut edges	*Lacking fibre*
TYPE 6	Fluffy pieces with ragged edges, mushy	*Diarrhoea*
TYPE 7	Watery, no solid pieces, entirely liquid	*Diarrhoea*

The first version of the scale only used words to describe the texture, colour and form of stools, but later a visual element was added to make it easier for doctors to ask their patients to classify the condition of their stools.

Initially it was hoped the scale could help to assess intestinal transit rate (the rate at which a stool moves through the body), but further trials questioned its validity on this point. The scale did, however, prove to be an extremely valuable diagnostic tool when talking to patients about their stools. As a result the scale is now used around the world, with a new version produced for use with children, to make talking about poo that bit easier.

Mohs scale

Friedrich Mohs (1773–1839) was a German geologist who specialized in mining. He developed the Mohs hardness scale in 1812. At that time most minerals were classified by their chemical composition, but this did not aid comparison and was not easy to do in the field. The idea of comparing minerals by their hardness had been around for hundreds of years. Pliny the Elder compared diamond and quartz based on their hardness in his book *Naturalis Historia* (77 CE); however, no one had yet created a scale. Mohs, using his extensive knowledge of minerals, selected ten exemplars of differing hardness to create an ordinal scale. Ordinal scales are based on natural ordered categories, but the distances or values between categories is not known. This means that the minerals are ordered in relation to each other, becoming harder as one moves up the scale. The ten-point scale (shown opposite) was simple to use, as an unknown mineral could be easily tested against the ten index minerals.

To test the hardness of an unknown mineral, geologists would often carry a case with an example of each mineral on the scale (except diamond, which is too valuable to include in most kits). To test for hardness a point from one mineral would be rubbed

MOHS NO.	MINERAL
1	Talc
2	Gypsum
3	Calcite
4	Fluorite
5	Apatite
6	Orthoclase feldspar
7	Quartz
8	Topaz
9	Corundum
10	Diamond

across a flat surface of another mineral to see if it produced a scratch. Should specimen *a* scratch specimen *b*, then specimen *a* is harder. If specimen *a* does not scratch specimen *b*, then specimen *b* is harder. If the two specimens are equal in hardness, then they will barely form a scratch on each other. Another way of testing a mineral in the field is to carry a kit of some standard objects for which you know the Mohs score; for example, a fingernail scores 2–2.5, a piece of glass 4–7, and a steel file 5–6.5. Later scales became more automated; for example, the Vickers scale, which was developed in 1921 and involves scratching the item to be tested with a diamond-tipped indenter with a set load for

10–15 seconds. The resultant indentation is then analysed microscopically to give a score on the scale. Although this is a more accurate measure of hardness than the Mohs scale, it requires laboratory conditions. The Mohs scale, on the other hand, can be easily deployed by amateurs, and as a result has retained its popularity as a basic measure of the hardness of minerals.

CONVERSION TABLES

STONES & POUNDS TO KILOGRAMS

There are approximately 2.2 pounds in 1 kilogram. To convert kilograms to pounds, multiply the number of kilograms by 2.2. If you wish to convert pounds to kilograms, divide by 2.2.

0 st 1 lb	0.453 kg	0 st 8 lb	3.628 kg
0 st 2 lb	0.907 kg	0 st 9 lb	4.082 kg
0 st 3 lb	1.360 kg	0 st 10 lb	4.535 kg
0 st 4 lb	1.814 kg	0 st 11 lb	4.989 kg
0 st 5 lb	2.267 kg	0 st 12 lb	5.443 kg
0 st 6 lb	2.721 kg	0 st 13 lb	5.896 kg
0 st 7 lb	3.175 kg	1 st 0 lb	6.350 kg

There are 30.48 cm to 1 foot. To convert centimetres to feet, divide the cm figure by 30.48. To convert feet to centimetres, multiply the feet figure by 30.48.

1 in	2.54 cm	20 in	50.8 cm
2 in	5.08 cm	25 in	63.5 cm
3 in	7.62 cm	30 in	76.2 cm
4 in	10.16 cm	35 in	88.9 cm
5 in	12.7 cm	40 in	101.6 cm
6 in	15.24 cm	45 in	114.3 cm
7 in	17.78 cm	50 in	127 cm
8 in	20.32 cm	55 in	139.7 cm
9 in	22.86 cm	60 in	152.4 cm
10 in	25.4 cm	65 in	165.1 cm
11 in	27.94 cm	70 in	177.8 cm
12 in	30.48 cm	75 in	190.5 cm
13 in	33.02 cm	80 in	203.2 cm
14 in	35.56 cm	85 in	215.9 cm
15 in	38.1 cm	90 in	228.6 cm
16 in	40.64 cm	95 in	241.3 cm
17 in	43.18 cm	100 in	254 cm
18 in	45.72 cm		
19 in	48.26 cm		

10 cm	0.328084 ft	0 ft 3.9 in
20 cm	0.656168 ft	0 ft 7.9 in
30 cm	0.984252 ft	0 ft 11.8 in
40 cm	1.3123 ft	1 ft 3.7 in
50 cm	1.6404 ft	1 ft 7.7 in
60 cm	1.9685 ft	1 ft 11.6 in
70 cm	2.2966 ft	2 ft 3.6 in
80 cm	2.6247 ft	2 ft 7.5 in
90 cm	2.9528 ft	2 ft 11.4 in
100 cm	3.2808 ft	3 ft 3.4 in
110 cm	3.6089 ft	3 ft 7.3 in
120 cm	3.937 ft	3 ft 11.2 in
130 cm	4.2651 ft	4 ft 3.2 in
140 cm	4.5932 ft	4 ft 7.1 in
150 cm	4.9213 ft	4 ft 11.1 in
160 cm	5.2493 ft	5 ft 3 in
170 cm	5.5774 ft	5 ft 6.9 in
180 cm	5.9055 ft	5 ft 10.9 in
190 cm	6.2336 ft	6 ft 2.8 in
200 cm	6.5617 ft	6 ft 6.7 in

MILES TO KILOMETRES

To convert from miles to kilometres, multiply your figure by 1.609344 (or divide by 0.62137119223733)

1 mi	1.6093 km	14 mi	22.53 km
2 mi	3.2187 km	15 mi	24.14 km
3 mi	4.828 km	16 mi	25.75 km
4 mi	6.4374 km	17 mi	27.36 km
5 mi	8.0467 km	18 mi	28.97 km
6 mi	9.6561 km	19 mi	30.58 km
7 mi	11.27 km	20 mi	32.19 km
8 mi	12.87 km	21 mi	33.8 km
9 mi	14.48 km	22 mi	35.41 km
10 mi	16.09 km	23 mi	37.01 km
11 mi	17.7 km	24 mi	38.62 km
12 mi	19.31 km	25 mi	40.23 km
13 mi	20.92 km	26 mi	41.84 km

COOKING: IMPERIAL & METRIC

½ oz	15 g	8 oz	227 g
1 oz	29 g	10 oz	283 g
2 oz	57 g	12 oz	340 g
3 oz	85 g	13 oz	369 g
4 oz	113 g	14 oz	397 g
5 oz	141 g	15 oz	425 g
6 oz	170 g	16 oz	453 g

COOKING: MEASURING VOLUME

⅟₁₆ cup	½ fl oz	15 ml	1 tbs
⅛ cup	1 fl oz	30 ml	2 tbs
¼ cup	2 fl oz	59 ml	4 tbs
⅓ cup	2½ fl oz	79 ml	5.5 tbs
⅜ cup	3 fl oz	90 ml	6 tbs
½ cup	4 fl oz	118 ml	8 tbs
⅔ cup	5 fl oz	158 ml	11 tbs
¾ cup	6 fl oz	177 ml	12 tbs
1 cup	8 fl oz	240 ml	16 tbs
2 cups	16 fl oz	480 ml	32 tbs
4 cups	32 fl oz	960 ml	64 tbs
6 cups	48 fl oz	1420 ml	96 tbs
8 cups	64 fl oz	1895 ml	128 tbs

NOTES

p. 4   Presidential Inaugural Address to the General
          Meeting of the British Association, Edinburgh, 2
          August 1871, in *Report of the Forty-First Meeting of the
          British Association for the Advancement of Science*, 1872,
          John Murray, London, p. xci.

p. 13   *Philebus* 55e, trans. R.W. Sharples.

p. 15   'Address to the Mathematical and Physical Sections
          of the British Association, Liverpool, 15 Sep 1870', in
          The Scientific Papers of James Clerk Maxwell, Cambridge
          University Press, 1890; Dover Publications, Mineola
          NY, 2003, vol. 2, p. 217.

p. 47   *The Garden of Epicurus* (1894), trans. Alfred Allinson,
          in *The Works of Anatole France in an English Translation*,
          The Bodley Head, London, 1920.

p. 105   Charles Babbage, Reflections on the Decline of
          Science in England, B. Fellowes, London, 1830.

p. 131   *Scientific Method: An Inquiry into the Character and
          Validity of Natural Laws*, Kegan Paul, London, 1923,
          p. 113.

p. 132   J. Gehrer (ed.), *Martha Lloyd's Household Book*,
          Bodleian Library Publishing, Oxford, 2021, p. 99.

p. 159   'The Significance of Quantitative Research in
          Physics', Inaugural Address at the University of
          Leiden (1882).

FURTHER READING

Jeanne Bendick, *How Much and How Many*, Brockhampton
    Press, Leicester, 1960.
A.E. Berriman, *Historical Metrology*, J.M. Dent, London, 1953.
Norman Biggs, *Quite Right: The Story of Mathematics,
    Measurement, and Money*, Oxford University Press, Oxford,
    2016.
Colin R. Chapman, *How Heavy, How Much and How Long?
    Weights, Money and Other Measures Used by Our Ancestors*,
    Lochin Publishing, Dursley, 1995.
Anita Ganeri, *From Cubit to Kilogram: The Story of Weights and
    Measures*, Evans Brothers, London, 1996.
Jan Gyllenbok, *Encyclopedia of Historical Metrology, Weights and
    Measures*, vol. 1, Birkhauser, Basel, 2017.
Edward Nicholson, *Men and Measures: A History of Weights and
    Measures, Ancient and Modern*, Smith, Elder, London, 1912.
Andrew Robinson, *The Story of Measurement*, Thames &
    Hudson, London, 2007.
F.G. Skinner, *Weights and Measures: The Ancient Origins
    and Their Development in Great Britain up to A.D. 1855*,
    Her Majesty's Stationery Office, London, 1967.
Thyra Smith, *The Story of Measurement*, Basil Blackwell,
    Oxford, 1959.
Ian Whitelaw, *A Measure of All Things: The Story of Measurement
    through the Ages*, David & Charles, Cincinnati OH, 2007.

IMAGES

INDEX